the
Gifted
Way
to
Manage
Your
Career

Also by James P. Barber

From New York to Indiana: A History of the Ira Barber Family Beginning in 1786

The Collector, the Guide and the Bone-Digger

The Gifted Way
to
Manage Your
Career

Grow and Sustain Your Career
through
The 5-Phase Career Model
and
Faith-Based Principles

James P. Barber

THE OTHER ROAD PUBLISHING

THE GIFTED WAY TO MANAGE YOUR CAREER

The Other Road Publishing, 630 Nancy Street, Warsaw, Indiana 46580

www.jamespbarber.com

Printed in the United States of America.

First Edition, 2015.

ISBN: 978-0692532393

This book is dedicated to my family, whom I too many times placed second to my duties at work. It is also dedicated to their families who now provide a tremendous joy to me in my retired years. Marti, Matt, Estera, Eliana, Josh, Vanessa, Jarod, Tyler, Sarah, Michael, Sydney, Macy, and Lindsay, I love you all!

CONTENTS

Acknowledgments

I would like to thank a longtime friend and colleague, Phil Zile, for his encouragement for this project and for his edit work on the book. Phil has been a trusted adviser for me in both my business life and my spiritual life.

There have been numerous people I have worked with and for in the course of my business career. They helped influence my abilities, my growth and my management style. I apologize to all those who had to endure my mistakes in the early years of my role as a leader. Please know that I did truly learn by my mistakes. You have all helped make me a better person. Thank you.

For more information on servant leadership as coined by Robert K. Greenleaf, please visit The Robert K. Greenleaf Center for Servant Leadership at www.greenleaf.org.

For more information regarding David Lockeretz photographs and hiking in southern California, please visit his blog at www.nobodyhikesin-la.com.

Preface

Every generous act of giving and every perfect gift is from above and comes down from the Father who made the heavenly lights, in whom there is no inconsistency or shifting shadow. In accordance with his will he made us his children by the word of truth, so that we might become the most important of his creatures (James 1:17-18 ISV).

I worked for a leading U.S. telecommunications company, Sprint Corporation, for 32 years. I owned my own business/technology business for nearly five years where I served as the VP-Marketing. I measured my life by my work and by my accomplishments at work. I received numerous accolades and awards for sales, project management, middle management successes, excellence in values and leadership.

I did not climb to the C-level at Sprint, but I provided very specific direction and guidance for those levels due to my commitment, integrity, trustworthiness and simple knack to get things done, and done well. I was at many times in my career charged with taking failing areas and restoring them to successful enterprises. I was also tapped to develop new areas of business with nationwide responsibilities. I was respected by my superiors, my colleagues and my subordinates.

I worked too many hours. I missed too many family meals. I worried too much about failure. I worried too much about success. I worried about the teams who worked for me. I worried about our customers. Yes, I was quite a worrier!

All along the way I endeavored to maintain my integrity, my honesty, my commitment and my ethical standards; I failed a couple of times. For a long time, my prayer life was mostly selfish and self-centered when it was anything at all. It was only about half-way through my career that I really began to rely on God. I had moved into a new sales management position. I was empowered to develop a team and the business direction in a new area for the company.

Here's the brief story that speaks to some of my strengths and weaknesses, successes and failures. I, along with several others, put together a unique team to handle sales, engineering, technical support, installation, and order processing. We had formed our own business within the business, and we did it very well. It couldn't have been more team-oriented. Unfortunately, as successful as we were, my immediate superior wanted more. He suggested we get more revenue by "cheating." I say cheating, but to him we were just working the system and taking advantage of its faults. It wasn't right. It didn't smell right, and it didn't feel right. I fought him for months. I finally gave in, but only after I put everything in writing making it very clear what was going on. I guess this made me feel like I was washing my hands of any responsibility for wrong-doing. I also told him that we would blow our objectives out of the water, and some large sales bonuses would be due. He thought that was all great.

At year's end, it was as I had predicted. Our sales numbers far exceeded expectations. As a result, I and some sales reps were due some substantial bonuses. My manager said that it would not look right to pay me that large of a bonus. I should not have been surprised by that. After fruitless arguing with him, I took my documentation to the vice-president, and ultimately I was paid. I then turned in my resignation. I had compromised my integrity. It had all sickened me.

I quit my job, and I had nothing to fall back on. So, I thought it would be a good time to start my own business. I love research; I love writing. I decided to look into becoming a freelance technical writer. At about the same time I was approached by three individuals, two of whom I had worked with previously, who wanted me to join them in a new business venture providing voice, data and video technology solutions for community banks.

I was really torn about what to do. I prayed about it for weeks. My confidence in myself was failing. I had quit my job with no plan. I felt lost. I did not know what to do. I began to fear trying to work at my own business. What was I thinking?! I prayed some more, "God, please tell me what to do! What job should I pursue!" This was not a good situation for a worrier like me. My prayers, they were all about me.

Then, one evening I was sitting quietly in a chair. I began to pray, but I just broke down in tears. I felt abandoned and alone. I felt like a total failure. I was at the bottom ... I was right where God wanted me. It was then that he spoke to me. It was not a booming voice nor a quiet whisper. But, I heard the words in my head as clearly as if someone were standing next to me. He said, "Jim, it doesn't matter what you do. I am with you always." Instantly, I felt a weight had been lifted from me. There was a peace that I had not experienced in a very long time.

I made a decision the next day to become a partner with those three other individuals. I truly do believe it would not have made any difference which way I decided, however. My role in this new business would allow me to use my talents, including my writing skills. A small business is great as you get to wear many hats. I was VP-Marketing. I provided all of our sales and collateral materials. I wrote the final draft of all of our customer proposals. I prepared a website. I also worked directly with customers in a consulting role after developing a unique business/technology integration plan.

I worked out of an office in my home, but my wife said I was late for supper more than I had been when I worked at Sprint. I traveled a lot; not great distances, but more than I enjoyed. Running your own business can be both exhilarating and all-consuming. After nearly five years I was burned out.

Some time later an opportunity came along for me to return to Sprint, not in the sales group. I became a project manager for large business customers throughout the state. There was a lot of responsibility and a lot of freedom. This eventually led to my managing a team of project managers. My past successes in fixing problems and developing new areas then took me into a role developing and managing a nationwide contractor program. After that I managed a wireless technical support team, and eventually all of the project management for large business customers for the eastern half of the United States.

I'll include some additional details on this story later in the book. I have also included a summary of my personal career in Appendix 2. So, okay, why did I tell you all of this? It was definitely not to brag. That is simply not my style. No, I want you to know three things:

One, I have the business experience to discuss the topic of this book. I have lived every bit of what I am talking about in these pages from a business and career perspective. What I am sharing is based upon experience, not classroom theories. I have been a strong individual contributor, a high-level team player, an effective team leader and an entrepreneurial middle manager at a major U. S. corporation. I have also run my own business in a highly successful manner having been recognized as one of the top 100 new small businesses in America by *Entrepreneur* magazine and Dun & Bradstreet in 1997.

Two, I have made enough mistakes to understand the things you are going to face in your own experience. It was not all success for me; I had failures. I learned by them, and so must you, for you will have failures. You need to see this as much a part of your growth as your successes are.

Three, I have not always demonstrated the values of a Christian in the way I lived my life. I wish I had, but the truth is that I did not. I recall attending church at about age five. The next time was with my wife (she was my girlfriend at the time) sometime after high school. I did not join a church until we were married. She was Catholic, so I became Catholic also. At that time, the Catholic Church was good for me as I needed lots of rules and regulations. Eventually, we both left the Catholic Church, and today we attend a non-denominational community church. My faith journey has been a long slow one. I feel I can share what I have learned with an understanding based on both what I have done right and what I did wrong for so many years. Again, I am sharing my real-world journey.

So, that's it about me. The rest of the book will be about you and your career journey. While directed at those entering a career for the first time, this book is also applicable to those changing careers or those re-entering the workforce. As with so many initiatives, there are those who do not fit within the dimensions of the program or process. I have found that the 80/20 rule is pretty accurate for many areas in business. That is, the system is applicable in about 80% of the cases; about 20% are exceptions to the rule. This book follows that 80/20 rule. I feel the content applies to 80% of those of you who are career minded. The other 20% fall to one side or the other of the simple Bell curve. Either they do not have enough interest in a career to follow this advice, or they are those geniuses who do not fit into the mold of a standard career path but rather create their own way, often outside of the norm. In all likelihood, if you are reading this book, then you fall within the 80%. This book is for you.

What this book is about is helping you understand the phases you will go through as you manage your career *in the manner that you want it to unfold.* I will recommend tools such as establishing your goals and learning to be a servant-leader. But, it is up to you to do your homework and to put in the time to build your own path to success. I hope to provide some guidance for you so you can see your path. Based on personal successes and failures, I will discuss these things in a real-world manner. That does not mean I did not take advantage of many great tools available or that you should not do the same. I am here to lend you a hand through my experience as a businessman and as a follower of the way of Christ. It is a journey that God wants to be involved in with you. Don't wait to let him in. Just welcome him and talk with him and share with him, and, yes, cry with him when needed. He is always there for you. You are important to him.

James P. Barber
2015

Introduction

For we are God's workmanship, created in Christ Jesus to do good works, which God prepared in advance for us to do (Ephesians 2:10 NIV).

The Gifted Way

You have a new career before you, perhaps as your first job, or perhaps as one who has changed jobs or companies or even careers. It is a new start that can seem both exciting and daunting. You obviously want to do your very best. You want to be successful! It is a natural part of each of us to desire success. Contrary to what some may want you to believe, success is not contrary to what God wants for you. Yes, success is okay. Now, how you handle success and what you do with it is another story. *So be careful how you live. Don't live like fools, but like those who are wise. Make the most of every opportunity in these evil days. Don't act thoughtlessly, but understand what the Lord wants you to do* (Ephesians 5:15-17 NLT).

We can honor our walk with God and our relationships with others in the way we conduct ourselves in our work. Part of that is understanding what God has planned for us. Some of you may feel that you have your lives together and know just where you are going. Others, like myself when I began my career, are only looking at the near-term and hoping to get through the next weeks and months and not make fools of ourselves in front of our new co-workers.

I want this book to be a tool for you to help you understand how to manage your career regardless of your present understanding of your plans for the future. I will show you five phases of your career that will help you to have an idea of where you are and what to expect. But, most importantly, underlying all of this will be a foundation of faith-based principles to support you in making good decisions. You will find that you will do some things right along the way, and you will make some mistakes along the way. Learning by your mistakes is one of the top lessons to learn.

But you must remain faithful to the things you have been taught. You know they are true, for you know you can trust those who taught you (2 Timothy 3:14 NLT). Those who taught you truth probably included not only your instructors, but also your parents, among others. You will likely test many of the things you were taught as you enter your career. You will encounter situations that you will not feel like you were totally prepared for. You will make those mistakes. Just remember that when you stay true to what is right, you can be firm in your position. When in doubt you can test what is right in this manner: *All Scripture is inspired by God and is useful to teach us what is true and to make us realize what is wrong in our lives. It corrects us when we are wrong and teaches us to do what is right* (2 Timothy 3:16 NLT).

Everyone of us has received a gift from God. We must all make a decision to accept or reject this gift. There is only one correct answer. It is in this gift that we find the truth. It is in this gift that we can find our way. Pursuing your career with the gift is the right way to do it. Your ultimate success is defined in your relationship with the gift. Knowing what God wants you to do with your life is not always easy to discern. And, oftentimes, just when we think we have it figured out, we are thrown a curve. Our success is a progressive journey; it is a system of growth. We begin as infants and progress along a winding path. *Jesus answered, "I am the way and the truth and the life. No one comes to the Father except through me"* (John 14:6 NIV).

God's son is the gift that is our way in the world, in our personal lives, in our relationships, in our failures, in our successes and, yes, in our careers. God has also gifted us with talents and keen minds and caring hearts. We can honor God when we let his gifts guide us in every facet of our daily conduct and our relationships with others.

Vision and Mission

I have developed vision and mission statements numerous times in my career. In fact, in my early days at United Telephone of Indiana, I was part of a small committee that developed the company's first such statements. I subsequently developed vision and mission statements for departments and teams as well as for my own business. I also developed a personal vision statement for myself in 1992. I have shared this as an example in **Appendix 4** as I think it is important for you to consider your own vision in life. Notice that I did not say a vision statement for your career. Your career is a part of your life, and how you conduct your life should be the foundation for how you see yourself developing your career.

A vision is the expected outcome that you foresee. It shows the potential that you see for the future of yourself, your team, your department, your division or your company. This is where you use a bit of your imagination to see the best possible outcome that could be. Sometimes your vision may need to look through barriers and overcome challenges. It should be empowering for you and your team, and it should set a direction and develop the passion that will drive you. And, finally, it should be based on your values, either your personal values or those of your organization. You need to understand your values very clearly in developing a personal vision statement. This takes some soul-searching on your part to know the real you, but it is a wonderful exercise to undertake.

With this said, here is my vision for this book:
- I want to share with you, and help you to understand, **The 5-Phase Career Model** that I have developed.
- I want you to see your career in terms of these five phases so that you can clearly understand your actions and reactions as your career develops.
- I want to provide faith-based principles as a foundation to guide you through the five phases.
- I want you to understand that you are in charge of managing your career, not someone else.
- I want you to be able to successfully begin, grow and sustain

your career to the ultimate fulfillment of your career goals.

A mission statement should be one simple statement that describes the ultimate goal or purpose and expresses the conviction to get there. It is a simple statement that expresses the vision that has been shared. I like the idea of a single sentence mission statement. It should express fulfillment of the vision statement in a clear manner. Oftentimes for a business, it is the single statement that you can easily share that describes your business. It is that "elevator statement" that you can share with a stranger who asks you what line of work you are in.

For this book then, our mission together is to help you successfully manage the The 5-Phase Career Model through the application of faith-based principles from your first day on the job to the ultimate fulfillment of your career goals.

About You

This book is written to provide direction for you in managing your business career from your first day on the job to the summit of your business career. The very foundation of everything you do in pursuit of a successful business career is based on the one and only truth. This guidance comes from The Way of Christ. Jesus' way is the one true and firm foundation to everything you do and everything you will become, not only in your personal life but also in your business life.

Before the first day of your business career, you were likely in some type of training situation, anything from university studies to technical school to self-study programs to immersed learning activities. You were building a foundation for your planned career, or at least the career you planned for yourself based upon your life experiences up to that point in your life.

Now, you may or may not currently have a God-based foundation in your personal life. And, if you do, your commitment to following The Way of Christ is as diverse as your personality is from that of others. So, let's examine how you can make use of the guidance provided by this book regardless of where you are in your faith journey.

First, perhaps you are not a believer in Jesus Christ as the Son of God. Well, I would hope that this book will help steer you in the direction of Christ if you are willing to have an open mind. I believe you will find that the simple faith-based principles used to guide you in managing your own business career form a solid foundation upon which to begin your future from day one on the job. These practical, common-sense truths will guide you well. They are sound. Even if you are not a Christian, these principles can be applied to great success in managing your number one business — *you*. And, just maybe, along the way you will begin to see the new life that Jesus offers to you.

Second, maybe you are at the very beginning of your journey with Christ. Maybe it was a family member or a good friend or some loved one who introduced you to Christ. You sort of liked what your heard, but you still have some questions and doubts (guess what, we all do) and you are just unsure. You fear the commitment that comes with really surrendering your life to a figure you don't know a lot about. You've dipped your toe in the water, but you are unsure about jumping in. Okay. Let's get to know him a little better. Let's see how he can help you grow and make sound business decisions that will allow you to manage and have some control over your business career. No one expects you to see a brilliant flash of light and suddenly change your life, although it has happened. Take your time and learn more about this man named Jesus.

Third, you might feel you have a firm understanding of and a commitment to God in your personal life. But, that's your personal life, and you feel you can't bring your personal life into your business life. You feel you need to keep them separate. I tell you that you will have a good deal of difficulty leading a double life. Managing your career with Christ doesn't mean you have to wear sack cloth and sandals at work or spout memorized Bible verses to your co-workers. I am talking about managing your business career with sound, solid, proven principles. There's plenty of room in business for honesty and integrity, and so much more. You can learn to live as well in your business life as you do in your personal life. How you share your faith with others is another issue entirely and has to be based not only on your own comfort level, but more importantly on the comfort level of others in their journey. This book is not about evangelizing. What you may find, however, is that by following these sound faith-based principles and developing a successful career, you may gain the attention of others (in a good way). Again, how you handle sharing that foundational faith with others is dependent upon you, the other individual and your relationship with that person.

Finally, maybe you are all in with Christ. You are a true follower of his way. That does not necessarily make you a good manager. You have many good tools at your disposal, but you need to know how to use them at the appropriate time and in the appropriate situation. In some regards, you may need to learn how to temper the use of your tools. You need to understand people and the management process. Each person you encounter in your career is a diverse individual at their own place on their personal career path as well as on their personal journey with Christ. Accordingly, you need to learn how to work with each person as the uniquely created child of God that they are.

Wherever you are in your walk with Christ, you probably feel that your training and education before entering the workforce will serve you well. If you have pursued a technical field, you likely feel pretty good about the technical training you received. If you have one or more university degrees, you certainly feel well-prepared to make your mark right away. Depending on how well you prepared and studied, you may have a great deal of confidence, or you may wish you had paid a little more attention in class. Hopefully, you are not of the mind-set that you are entitled to a high-paying, upper-level position since you have done all the required training and attained fairly good grades. If this is your frame of mind, you need to step back for a minute.

First of all, you are not entitled to anything. I don't care what school you attended, what degree you attained, how hard you studied or how good your grades were, *you are not entitled*. You are just beginning your career. You are just beginning the next phase of your education, if you will. Sorry to knock you off your high horse, but this is that thing that people call the "real world." Welcome to it. Join the rest of us. (Now, I will admit that there are exceptions. In all likelihood, however, you are not one of them.)

I began my career as a computer programmer. Now, come on, in today's world that's certainly no big deal. Students can develop code. I will admit that this was some time ago for me. Still, I knew several computer languages, and I had even done some work for the university in one of their business schools. I was ready to go. My first day at work, I was placed alone in a conference room and handed numerous large IBM manuals and told to study them. Wait, studying on my first day of work?! Well, I discovered there was a lot in those manuals that I did not understand. In fact, when I finally got around to working on my first computer program in the real business world, I had to ask for help in how to assign the types of resources I had never used in the university setting. Oh, the shame!

So, get humble. Sure, you have learned a lot. Good that you have confidence in your abilities. Good that you are ready to go. Also be ready to continue your education. Be able to put your pride behind you. You will never stop learning. The day you think you have nothing else to learn is the day to do some serious re-evaluation of yourself. Before day one on the job, be ready to be humbled.

Did you take a class in business ethics? Well, maybe it was mentioned in some course in passing. We never had such a class; there were ethics classes, but nothing specific to business ethics. If you had a business ethics class, how seriously was it taken? Were jokes made about ethics in the business world? Perhaps you are of the mind-set that all big businesses are unethical. Did you consider business ethics when you interviewed for your job? If ethics in business are important to you, and they should be, hopefully you did consider this. What if you did not take this into consideration and you find yourself working for a company whose ethics are an affront to you. What do you do? Well, if this is a real issue and you know it before the first day on the job, you can graciously back out of the job. Wow, now that's tough since you had many interviews and not a lot of job offers. That puts a bit of a cramp in your situation. There is, however, another approach to take. Some would consider it to be "tilting at windmills." You can go to work for the company and be the most ethical person you can be. You can try to influence others by your ethics. Maybe you can plan one day to rise to a level where you can make real and lasting change. Wow, quite a challenge for a first job!

To some degree, you might realize that you are going to be introduced to ethical issues wherever you work. Just because a company is in an ethical business does not mean that the company operates in an ethical manner. Unless the company has such a reputation, you may not realize it until after you have worked there for a while. Again, you need to be strong enough to maintain your own ethics and maybe even try to influence others. This can be a real challenge. You may find yourself learning through the school of hard knocks in your first job. You know right from wrong, and you are going to need a lot of strength and sound guidance to work through the situation.

Let's talk a moment about what your expectations were for your first position. This is something that has changed greatly from the time when I first entered the workforce. Business thrived after World War II and into the 1960s and 1970s. Loyalty was a big issue. When you went to work for a company, you were expecting to make a lifetime career at that company. Similarly, the company was expecting that you would make your career with them, and they would do what they needed in order to keep you in their employ. You looked for a company in your chosen field that suited your needs to provide for your family until the day you retired. You looked for a company that cared for its employees and had high ethical standards. And, they existed.

There are still good companies with high ethical standards who value their employees. But, generally, there has been a shift in the loyalty department. It is a bit trite, but for many companies employees have become numbers to be used until they no longer need them. Employees are easily discarded. Those remaining are told to "work smarter, not harder." With the loss of company loyalty came a similar shift in employee loyalty. Employees now see a job as a means to pay the bills and gain experience to move on to the next better paying job at the next company. Job hopping is the new normal. The median number of years that wage and salary workers had been with their current employer was 4.6 years in January 2014, unchanged from January 2012, according to the U.S. Bureau of Labor Statistics.

So, back to the question of what it is you are looking for in your first position. Is it just experience so you can move on? Or, do you want to learn and grow and contribute? And even if you then do move on, haven't you at least grown and just maybe made a bit of a difference to even one person? Also, who knows, you may want to come back to work at this company again some day.

You really need to know yourself. You do have gifts and talents to share with others. How do you want to use them? You have standards. Do you want to lower them? Do you want to lift others up? It can't be all about you. You have the job. Now go make something of it in the best possible way that you can!

What This Book Is Not

Let's talk about some things this book is not. There has been much written on how to allow God into your life. While, generally, how to be a better person through a personal relationship is a great thing, there is little that directly addresses letting God guide you in your work life as well. It is not that the principles are any different, it is more a matter of understanding how to apply them in this aspect of your life. That is what this book *is* about.

This is not a book on how to run a Christian-based business. Again, there are some good books available for that very purpose. This book is to help you manage you in *your business world*, in *your career* with God as the center. You may one day run your own business. The principles used to manage your career will easily apply.

There are tools easily available to evaluate yourself, to understand your strengths and weaknesses. This book is not about self-evaluation so much as it is about how to let faith guide you on this lifetime journey that is your career. It is good and valuable to understand as much as you can about yourself. It is something you should consider doing on a regular basis throughout your career. Locate those tools and take advantage of them.

There are plenty of high-quality books by great authors with a lot of research to guide you in the process of leadership, and especially servant-leadership. This book is not specifically about how to become that servant-leader; although, it is something you should strive for. I am not going to repeat the tried and true methods involved in this pursuit, but I will discuss the topic. This is really one of those things for you to dig into and practice. This book is about guiding you in your career using sound faith-based principles. Yes, servant-leadership is one of those key principles, and it is something you must practice to achieve your goals. This you must do, and you must put in the effort to do it.

Let's talk about your goals. Again, there are plenty of good tools available to help you establish your personal and professional goals. So, do your homework. Written goals are an essential part of your plan to success. To manage your career properly you must set goals and evaluate your progress. Can your goals change along the way? Of course they can! That is why you evaluate them and re-establish them from time to time. Yes, this management of your career takes some hard work!

Job Versus Career

Finally, I want to take just a moment to discuss the difference between a job and a career. You may be in a job and feel that it is no more than that. You may not see it as a career. A job can become a career if you want it to be. Here is how the *Merriam-Webster Dictionary* defines a job: "the work that a person does regularly in order to earn money." They define a career as "a field for or pursuit of consecutive progressive achievement especially in public, professional, or business life." Are you in your job just to earn money, or do you see it as a path to progressive achievement? This does not mean you have to set your sites on being the president of the company. You will evaluate, define and re-evaluate your own goals for achievement.

When I entered my first *job* out of college, I was interested in settling down in my new home with my wife and the baby that would arrive in a few months. I just wanted to do the best I could at being a programmer and being a contributor to society at large. I was happy to be done with school and to be working. I was happy to be an adult. I was happy to be able to provide for my family.

It was only after some time that I even thought about my *job* as a *career*. So, at some point, I made the decision that I was in a career and not a job. I began to set goals for myself. I began to see that I had the potential to do more and be more than what I perceived as my job. It became about growth and progression. And, it became about using the gifts and talents with which I was blessed.

You may feel that you only want to be the best at your particular new position that you can be. You may not see yourself as entering a management role in the future. A career does not necessarily mean a management career, although it is typically thought of in that manner of progression. I will help you to see that through **The 5-Phase Career Model**, you can progress as your gifts and talents allow you. Regardless of your career goals, there are defined phases that can guide you. So, let's get started!

1

The Basics

For the law was given through Moses; grace and truth came through Jesus Christ (John 1:17 NIV).

In Pursuit of Your Purpose

You may have just completed four years or more of university study. Perhaps, you have just graduated from a technical school or a trade school. Or, maybe you have completed a self-study or an immersed learning program. Whatever your situation, you have completed the preparation to begin a career in your chosen field. You probably feel like you put a lot of time and effort into the preparation. You may have had to work a job while attending school. It was difficult to maintain the energy and the focus. Maybe you have completed a mentorship or residency program that immersed you into your field of study and work and provided good insight for your future. You have put in your time, and you are ready. Maybe it was two years or four years or six years. Some days it felt like a lifetime.

Well, it was a small part of the preparation God planned for you a very long time ago. His workmanship is in you. He has prepared the way for you. He has big things in store for you. Are you on the same page? You have been given particular interests and talents and gifts. You chose your career because of those inherent attributes, among others. Maybe you have given a lot of thought to your purpose in life, maybe you are still trying to figure out your purpose, or maybe you have not given it much thought at all. Because you were created by God with your personality, with your specific set of characteristics, gifts, and talents, it might serve you well in better understanding your purpose to develop a relationship with him. He wants you to use your abilities and skills and talents to be successful in all areas of your life, including your work. In fact, it may be in your profession that he has his biggest plans for you.

Success can be meaningless without purpose. Let's look first at the Big Purpose. God wants us to know him, to have a relationship with him and to enjoy him. We were created to have joy and peace and love in our relationship with him. Of course, we have the free will not to pursue this relationship with God. But through him we have been given the opportunity to bear fruit. Our Big Purpose is our role as a child of God created by him to share in his blessings.

As unique individuals, we each have a special purpose in life. It may not be that specific job that you just found. It is, rather, a specific calling, a way to use the gifts and talents that you have. Your purpose is not fame or fortune or power. These may well be aspects of your life, and there is nothing inherently wrong with any of them. Your purpose will be served in how you use your achievements.

How we handle the expression of our purpose is up to each of us; this is the free will that we have to pursue good, or not, in our lives. It is important to be guided by the foundational rules we will look at shortly. We should not be guided by our own set of rules, which may seem good, but which are often self-centered at best. By trusting in a higher power, and our Big Purpose, we can better understand our individual purpose.

Of course, the universal question is, "How do I find my purpose in life?" Well, there are plenty of tools available to help with this, such as personality assessments. A few I have used include the Myers-Briggs Type Indicator®, the DiSC® Profile, and the Hogan Personality Inventory. There are plenty of authors with books to assist you. Some are life-based, and some are faith-based. One faith-based source that I found personally very helpful is *The Purpose Driven Life* by Rick Warren. It is one of those books that requires you to do a lot of work. Any good tool you use to find out more about yourself and your purpose is going to require you to put in some time and effort.

This may be one of those areas that you need to pursue on your own. Perhaps a trusted adviser or even the human resources department at you company can provide some direction. Some caution should be taken as, while there is plenty of literature available on this topic, some of it is pop psychology. So use common sense and recommendations you know are trusted. But surely, do not forget about the Big Purpose, and first develop a relationship with your creator.

Another approach is to simply review key events in your life. Now, depending on your age and life experiences, this may provide limited insight. Pay attention to how you responded to those events in your life. What strengths did you exhibit? How did others react to your response to a particular situation? Where did you fall down? What did you learn? How would you react to a similar situation in the future?

As you grow through life experiences and your relationship with God and find yourself at a new stage in life, you may see a new purpose. That is not uncommon. You may even find yourself developing in areas of weakness, leading you to new opportunities. You see, finding your purpose in life is a lifelong quest.

So, at this point, let's take a moment and talk about your influencers up to now. Let's look at how those around you have played a role in helping you to find your purpose. Certainly your parents played a key role in providing direction for your life, instilling in you the morals and attitudes that you have today. Sure, at some point, if you were like most young people, you blew them off as being too controlling or not understanding, or simply plain stupid. As you grow, however, you will see some of the good that they instilled in you.

I know there are exceptions to all of this. Let's face it, there are broken homes, there are broken people. Some overcome a bad childhood and make a good way for themselves. Some, unfortunately, do not and spend their lives unforgiving and living in bitterness. But, forgiveness is a real key to putting yourself on the right path.

You also had teachers and instructors in your life. Some were good, some were bad. Perhaps your choice of career was influenced by someone in this position. That is not unusual. Most of those in this position will see your talents and your strengths and steer you in a direction that makes good use of them. You may easily recall a teacher or a professor or a counselor who helped you find your way.

If you are married, then there is the influence of your spouse. Married, you have someone other than yourself to consider. You may even have children. They provide a great influence on you and the choices you make.

Of course, there are your friends. In our younger years, these friends can have a great deal of influence on us. Peer pressure is awfully intense. Your strength of character determined how much of an influence, good or bad, they had upon you.

There are others in your life — aunts, uncles, grandparents, mentors, coaches and pastors just to name a few. All of these people have helped you to grow into who you are today. But, remember, it is God who has always known who you are and who you can be. *Before I formed you in the womb I knew you, before you were born I set you apart* (Jeremiah 1:5 NIV). Additionally, *For we are his workmanship, having been created in Christ Jesus for good works that God prepared beforehand so we may do them* (Ephesians 2:10 NET). Yes, while there are many people in our lives influencing us along the way, God has always had a plan for each of us. Those people were under his direction and there for his purpose, just as you are. Do you want to know your purpose in life? Get to know God.

While these were all important things to consider, your first-time career decision has been made and is behind you. It is time to move forward with excitement and enthusiasm. You worked hard for this moment. So, let's take a look at some basics that will prepare you for success in your chosen profession. These will be foundational no matter what phase of your career you are in. They are as fundamental in nature through all phases of **The 5-Phase Career Model**, which we will look at in the next chapter, as they are in your life in general. Who you are and how you handle yourself is not divided into your personal life and your professional life. These basics are simply foundational to life. Now, if you are not a Christian, or maybe still on the fence, I hope you will give this a chance. While these fundamentals have a Judeo-Christian origin, they are found throughout our society and throughout the world. Even if you are not a follower of Christ these fundamentals are a real part of your life. So, please read on.

The Ten Critical Foundational Rules

We get all the basic instructions for living from the words spoken by God to Moses in Exodus 20. These tenets have been the foundation for living a God-honoring life. They provide a code of conduct, define the boundaries for moral living, and set-up a foundation for societal interaction.

Obviously the **Ten Critical Foundational Rules** that follow are better known as the *Ten Commandments*. A rule is "a prescribed guide for conduct or action" (*Merriam-Webster*). A commandment is "an important rule given by God that tells people how to behave" (*Merriam-Webster*). Various synonyms for both words have some commonality. So, we refer to these particular rules as commandments since they came from God.

In Jewish rabbinical tradition, the Torah contains 613 commandments, know as *mitzvot*. Further, the list of ten varies slightly between

Jewish, Catholic and Protestant faiths. Some Jewish resources note that these are ten categories for the full 613 *mitzvot*. Jewish tradition, as well as some Protestant traditions, hold that the first five rules reference duties to God, and the second five rules reference duties to people. This division seems obvious with perhaps the exception of number five, honor your father and mother. However, again according to some traditions, your birth is held as the divine work of God and is, thus, a God-honoring duty. Others view the fifth rule as a transition linking the first four to the last five (Judaism 101 2015 and Hebrew for Christians 2015).

Another interesting note is that the commandments are not really referenced as such when they are first presented by Moses. As previously noted, the Jewish rabbinical tradition has 613 commandments, or *mitzvot*. In the original Hebrew text, however, the commandments are referenced by a different word that can mean word, speak or thing. So, these might be more specifically defined as the Ten Words. We can further note that after Moses went up to the mountain the second time to speak with God and received the commandments, he returned to the people and said, *And God spoke all these words* (Exodus 20:1 NIV). Most English translations I reviewed had a similar translation; the word commandment is not used (Judaism 101 2015 and Hebrew for Christians 2015).

However you look at these words, as a Jew, Catholic or Protestant, they were provided as sound rules to live by. And even if you are a non-believer, maybe you can ignore the first four rules, but the remaining six are foundational to living a moral life, a giving and serving life, and a loving life. For your ease of reference I have summarized these **Ten Rules**, along with some specific actions, in **Appendix 1, The Ten Rules in Action in Your Career**.

Excerpted from Exodus 20 (NIV):

> **Rule 1**: *I am the Lord your God, who brought you out of Egypt, out of the land of slavery. You shall have no other gods before me.*
> We must honor God at all times. It was he who brought us

to this point in our lives. He has blessed us with rich blessings, with gifts and talents. He provided guides in our lives to help us. We must never forget the source of all that we are and all that we can be. He is the ultimate boss in our career wherever we are.

What other gods might be before you? Money, glory, fame, sex, lust, and control to name a few. When you set your career goals, which of these other gods came to mind as you planned your future? Are you in this just to make money and gain more stuff? Are you in it to show others that you have made it big? Maybe you want to rub it in the face of those who said you couldn't make it. Now, you can see your name with a big title in front of it or with letters behind it. You tell yourself that titles and positions make you attractive. The opposite sex will be drawn to you. Even if you don't commit adultery, the lust might be satisfying. Maybe it all comes down to the power and control you will have over others. If any of these idols are your reason for pursuing your career goals, you need to step back and get in touch with the one true God. Seek out a trusted friend or loved one to discuss this with. Seek counseling if you cannot talk to someone you know. In any case, you really need to understand your reasons for your goals. Ultimately, it comes down to living a life that is God-honoring. We will see how this applies as we move forward.

Rule 2: *You shall not make for yourself an image in the form of anything in heaven above or on the earth beneath or in the waters below. You shall not bow down to them or worship them; for I, the Lord your God, am a jealous God.*

As we discussed with regard to **Rule 1**, you cannot pursue those other gods, those idols, in any way, shape or form.

Rule 3: *You shall not misuse the name of the Lord your God, for the Lord will not hold anyone guiltless who misuses his name.*

When is it we are most tempted to use the name of God in vain? It is when we are angry. As you manage yourself, and at some point others, you must be able to control your anger. You are going to be placed in situations where someone has put you in a bad position or even lied about you. You will need to know how to handle these situations without anger. If you are one who is prone to being easily angered, then maybe you need to consider anger management counseling. There is nothing wrong with doing this, and it is not a sign of weakness. On the contrary, it shows that you are strong enough and care enough for yourself and for others to take affirmative action to fix a recognized problem.

But, this rule also has to do with your relationship with the one who knew you before you were born. Do you honor and love this relationship enough to not misuse his name? Remember the Big Purpose is to know him and love him and live in joy and peace. Misusing his name is simply not in line with your Big Purpose.

Rule 4: *Remember the Sabbath day by keeping it holy. Six days you shall labor and do all your work, but the seventh day is a sabbath to the Lord your God.*

Well, that's pretty plain. Our society has pretty much tossed this one aside, however. It is refreshing to see businesses like Chik-fil-A and Hobby Lobby who close on Sundays. They give all of their employees the opportunity to rest from their work on that day. And, these businesses are still successful. There are so many stories of successfully run Christian-based businesses. You might want to study them. Now, maybe you work for a company that does operate on Sundays. Well, the point is to take some time off, and to use some of that time to honor God, even if it cannot be on Sunday. Time away from your job is important. It allows you to recharge your batteries and to focus on the other important aspects of your life.

Rule 5: *Honor your father and your mother.*

Family is so important. You put in a lot of hard work to get to this point in your career. You cannot forget those who helped you, who maybe provided guidance for you along the way. Maybe it wasn't your father and mother; maybe it was an aunt or uncle or close friend or spouse. Do not forget your roots. Living a God-honoring life in all aspects will do this. And, how about honoring those who have provided you with your job? How? By following all of the rules in your workplace. By doing your best and being your best.

Rule 6: *You shall not murder.*

Hopefully, you are not tempted to murder a fellow employee or a boss! But Jesus commented on this commandment, *But I tell you that anyone who is angry with a brother or sister will be subject to judgment* (Matthew 5:22 NIV). We discussed anger with regard to Rule 3 previously. This is a further, and perhaps more direct and personally stronger, admonishment.

Rule 7: *You shall not commit adultery.*

We are getting into some areas of temptations that you will be exposed to in the business environment. As Jesus said about this one, *But I tell you that anyone who looks at a woman lustfully has already committed adultery with her in his heart* (Matthew 5:28 NIV). Come on, now, this is being pretty tough on us isn't it, Jesus? No, he really understands the broken human condition. You may end up working very closely with someone of the opposite sex. Now, if you are unmarried and seeking a relationship, an attraction can be very normal. Care still needs to be taken in the workplace. But, if you are married, this is a huge red flag to watch for. If you are having feelings you should not, seek prayer and counsel. Understand your blessings.

Some companies do not allow the opposite sexes to travel alone together. Perhaps this is not a bad idea. Single or married, being alone together in a far-away place sharing meals, and maybe drinks, can be a potential formula for putting yourself in a tenuous position at best.

Rule 8: *You shall not steal.*

Here is another one of those temptations that is present in the workplace. It can't be stealing to take some pens or pencils home for your kids. Or, maybe a pad of paper. Others do it. They have even told you to go ahead since everyone does it. This can be a real slippery slope. Next, you will hear about "fudging" on your expense reports. Everybody does it. "We aren't given a proper allowance for travel anyway. This is how we make up some money we should have gotten." Or, maybe you have to turn in a time sheet to get paid. Adding a few extra hours seems okay from time to time. After all, you do work hard. There is also the stealing of time from your employer. How is that? By spending time on the internet for personal reasons when you should be working.

No, stealing is stealing. What did Jesus say about taking pencils home? *Whoever can be trusted with very little can also be trusted with much, and whoever is dishonest with very little will also be dishonest with much* (Luke 16:10 NIV). Okay, he didn't really say pencils, but I think you get the point (pun intended).

Sometimes God uses small things to test our integrity. It is those small, incidental choices of life where doing the right thing even when no one is looking that build character, the character that creates a real leader.

Rule 9: *You shall not give false testimony against your neighbor.*

Okay, you should have learned this one in kindergarten: do not lie. You don't lie about the work you have done; you do not take credit for someone else's work. You do not lie about someone to get back at them for something they did to you. You do not cover up a problem with your product or service. You do not mislead customers about your product by "stretching the truth." You better get this one, and you better see how it applies to your career. But, you say, you know people who have lied their way to a lucrative position. Yep, it has happened. I have seen it happen. But, you know, at some point those people seem to drift away from the company and maybe from some good relationships. I don't think it was all roses for them.

Rule 10: *You shall not covet your neighbor's house. You shall not covet your neighbor's wife, or his male or female servant, his ox or donkey, or anything that belongs to your neighbor.*

Has the American marketing message reached you? Do you want more? Do you want what someone else has? Are you told, and do you buy into, the message that you are entitled to have what others have? Wake up! It's simply not true and not right.

In your career, you will see others who make more money than you for doing similar work. You will be passed over for a promotion that you know that you deserved. You will be asked to do more than someone else. Life is not fair; business is not fair. Learn to live with what you have. Work hard for what you want. Oh, you have, and that other person still got the promotion. Why? If it is that important, talk to your boss. Find out in what areas you need to improve. Work with her to develop a plan to advance. And, of course, remember that God has a plan for you. Ask him to help you understand his plan for you. Ask, and then listen. Then listen some more.

The Gift

So, these words, rules and commandments provide a great guideline for living. They were provided to a confused and frightened people in need of direction. I think it is interesting to note that there are no punishments identified for violation of these words. These are truly guiding principles with rewards to follow for those who abide by them.

The way I see it, these words were a gift from God to a people in need. Or maybe more properly said, these words *are* a gift from God to *his people*. Period. We learn later in the New Testament that the Word became flesh in the birth of Jesus. And the Word Jesus was God's ultimate gift to all who believe. I do not think it is an accident that the Ten Commandments are perhaps more literally known to be the Ten Words. God's Word is a true gift to his people — yesterday, today and tomorrow. And using his gift, we can steer the course of all facets of our lives. There should be no difference in our actions in our daily personal lives versus our daily business lives. We are all people in need in some way; we are all his people.

The gift of God's Word is manifested through our actions: *But the fruit of the Spirit is love, joy, peace, forbearance, kindness, goodness, faithfulness, gentleness and self-control. Against such things there is no law* (Galatians 5:22-23 NIV). In the workplace, as well as in our personal lives, these gifts are revealed in our honesty, integrity, ethics, servanthood and chastity.

The 10:1 Factor in Action

These **Ten Rules** have been a solid foundation for societies throughout history. Yes, they have also been questioned by many throughout history. The Pharisees tried to trip Jesus up by asking him which of these **Ten Rules** was the greatest. So it has been throughout history as we tried to pick and choose those that we can really live by — you know, just a little compromise. Come on, if we had to live by just one, what would it be? But Jesus provided the answer, *"Teacher, which is the greatest commandment in the Law?" Jesus replied: "Love the Lord your God with all your heart and with all your soul and with all your mind. This is the first and greatest commandment. And the second is like it: Love your* *neighbor as yourself"* (Matthew 22:36-39 NIV).

So, there you have it, the ten boiled down to one … well two. But, he said the second is just like the first. If we love God with all of our heart, mind and soul, surely we will love others completely. So, what does this look like in the workplace?

Basic Behaviors

Let's talk about how these rules for living apply in managing your career. Let's start with honesty, integrity and ethics. *Merriam-Webster* defines ethics as "moral principles that govern a person's or group's behavior." Integrity is defined as "the quality of being honest and having strong moral principles; moral uprightness." If we are God-honoring, then we will be guided by these moral principals without compromise. You will not steal, cheat, lie or deceive to make a sale, look good in a meeting, gain an advantage, get a promotion, or for any other reason. These things are not acceptable in any manner. Period. Your entire reputation is at stake. Later, I'll share a couple of examples in my own career. For now, remember, *Choose a good reputation over great riches; being held in high esteem is better than silver or gold* (Proverbs 22:1 NLT). And, there is no reason to be deceptive: *All you need to say is simply 'Yes' or 'No'; anything beyond this comes from the evil one* (Matthew 5:37 NIV). Your "yes" should mean "yes," and your "no" should mean "no."

Here is a general example of a situation in which I guarantee you will be placed. Someone is going to come to you with a question that is of great importance to them. They are coming to you out of some degree of respect for your abilities and knowledge. They ask you the question, and you do not know the answer. Now, you don't want to look stupid, especially if there are others around. You are concerned about losing face, or perhaps that this individual and others will lose confidence in you. Since you do have some idea of what this person is asking about, you make up an answer that you think is probably right based upon the limits of what you do know. It is not really a lie, but it is not likely a low-risk answer because of your limitations. Anyway, how badly will it be if this answer is not correct? You see that it will be a good learning experience for this individual. It will make him do his homework more thoroughly next time. He will learn to better rely upon himself. Why, you are doing him a real favor by taking a guess! Anyway, you don't want to share too much of your knowledge; you have been told that knowledge is power.

Sorry. The best answer you could have provided is, "I don't know." Sure, you can follow-up with what you may know about the issue, but be clear that it is only a best guess based on your limits. Further, you may be able to suggest someone who does know. You will find over time that a "don't know" answer will be seen as one facet of your ethics and integrity. People will respect you for your honesty. You may even go so far as to follow up your "don't know" answer with, "... but let me find out for you." The only caution with this is that there are those people who will try to take advantage of you. They are lazy and will take the easy way. You will know who these people are over time, and you can simply leave it at "don't know."

You should also not look down on that person who needs your help. This is how you grow as a servant and as a leader. A servant is there to help. A leader is there, in part, to provide direction and guidance. A mature handling of the situation will pave your way to leadership.

As we will see in the next chapter, leadership is a large part of any career path. That is one reason there are so many books written on the topic. You can be a leader without being in an official supervisory or management position. When I first read of the concept of servant-leadership, I realized I was already practicing it; I just did not realize it since I was not aware of a name for it. I honestly do not recall which book I first read on the topic. There are plenty of good books on the topic. Ken Blanchard is one of many authors who comes to mind. The connection to the 10:1 answer given by Jesus is that as a servant-leader you are considering others (your neighbor who just happens to be someone who works for you or with you) first. You treat your team members as you would want to be treated. The concept is highlighted in this passage, ... *whoever wishes to be great among you must be your servant, and whoever wishes to be first among you must be your slave* (Matthew 20:26-27 NRSV). A servant-leader is focused on others.

In addition to mentioning honesty, integrity, ethics and servanthood in the earlier section, **The Gift**, I also mentioned chastity. That may seem like a strange word to use as one of the basics in your business career. Let's go back to see what *Merriam-Webster* has to say. Chastity is defined as "purity in conduct and intention; restraint and simplicity in design or expression." When your intentions are pure, you have the needs of others in mind when you make decisions. You are not making decisions out of malice or revenge. You will run into people who exhibit malice and revenge in their decision-making process. That is no way to manage your career. No, using restraint is the better way to go.

Then, of course, there is chastity in the more common thought of being chaste in sexual relations. Just remember to be cautious when working with the opposite sex. We talked about this when we took a look at **Rule 7**. Yes, chastity may seem like an outmoded word in today's society, but in several ways it is appropriate as a basic behavior in the workplace.

Finally, think about having balance in your life. You cannot honor God by not taking care of yourself. You cannot perform well if you are not well rested, both physically and mentally. There is nothing wrong with working hard, but there is something wrong with overworking yourself to the detriment of your health and your family. *Do not be anxious about anything, but in every situation, by prayer and petition, with thanksgiving, present your requests to God. And the peace of God, which transcends all understanding, will guard your hearts and your minds in Christ Jesus* (Philippians 4:6-7 NIV). One way to honor God and care for yourself is through daily prayer, and we will discuss more about this later as well.

Balance also means taking care of your family. You may have a commitment as a spouse or parent. You cannot ignore your family. Yes, it is a balancing act that seems overwhelming at times, especially when things are not going so well, either at work or at home. But as much as you want to have a successful career, do you really want that at the expense of those you love? Maybe it has reached a point where counseling is needed. If so, then go for it. There is no shame in working with a counselor. Most churches can support you with this process if needed.

Here's a brief story on one way I tried to maintain some semblance of balance with my family while dealing with a new position. I had taken a move into the network department at United Telephone of Indiana where I had the responsibility to bring into operation a couple of mini-computer systems that would monitor the telecommunications network statewide. The department had purchased the systems, but they had no one to get them up and running. It sounded like a nice challenge to me — a great learning opportunity. I had not worked with mini-computers, the operating systems they ran, nor the computer languages they used. There was a lot for me to learn in a very short time to meet the objectives for functional operation.

We had three children by this time ages eight, three and less than a year. Working overtime was limiting to family time and would also be a great burden on my wife. But, I really needed to spend the extra hours to achieve the goal that was expected of me. So, I made a bit of a compromise. I came home each night right after work so I could be with my family. Once all the kids were put to bed, I went back to work and worked some long hours late into the night. To me, it was one way to maintain some balance to meet my work objectives while still spending quality time with my family. It was not something I would do long-term, but it got me through the initial quick learning curve that I had to face in my job. Yes, you will sometimes need to make some personal sacrifices to maintain that work-family balance.

Another way to think about balance is with service in the community where you live. Offering to use your gifts and talents to the good of others in your church or community can be very rewarding while taking your mind away from your business problems. Many people find that they get answers to their problems merely by working in a group or on a project involving the needs of others. Relaxing your mind from your business can help open new ways to view a problem.

Balance is key to living a rewarding and fulfilling life. You are not just one facet of your life. You are more than a spouse or a mother or a father. You are more than a member of some organization. You are more than a good friend. You are more than your hobbies. You are more than your work. You are all of these things, and they all work together to make you a better person. Sure, you spend more time on some aspects of your life than others, but they are the ingredients of your life that you can mix to arrive at the right flavor. You need all of them.

Now, if thinking about work and family and friends and service seems a bit overwhelming, then do not forget about prayer. See, it was so easy to let that facet slip to the background. It should be in the fore-front. A daily prayer habit will provide tremendous sustenance to your life. For now, just realize that daily prayer does not have to be about memorized prayers and verses. One of the most fulfilling and soothing and relaxing forms of prayer that I try to do daily is to simply sit and listen to God. It is simply developing a relationship with him. With a good relationship, you can go to him for guidance in good times and bad. Establishing that relationship takes a commitment. It takes time, but it does not need to take a lot of time daily. Think about beginning your day spending five or ten or fifteen minutes just building that rela-tionship by simply being still and quiet, and listening.

Finally, brothers and sisters, whatever is true, whatever is noble, what-ever is right, whatever is pure, whatever is lovely, whatever is admirable — if anything is excellent or praiseworthy — think about such things (Philip-pians 4:8 NIV).

2

The 5-Phase Career Model

To every thing there is a season, and a time to every purpose under the heaven (Ecclesiastes 3:1 KJV).

Why?

It is perhaps understated to say that there has been much written about careers. For the most part, the authors of those books generally talk about three phases: 1) an early phase when you are still learning and full of potential, 2) a middle phase when you are applying your knowledge and moving forward with experience, and 3) a final phase where you have either charged fully and confidently ahead as a leader, or you have passed your most effective years and are in a decline. You basically go from a growth phase and into a mature phase through gains in your knowledge and experience. This would not be a misleading representation of a career; however, I feel it leaves out some important issues, challenges, questions and opportunities you will face in your career development.

While your age and experience are key factors in your career, there are other influences and challenges you will meet in the workplace along the way that will help to shape you. There are contributions you will make that will influence your growth and advancement. How these will be viewed may be very different depending upon where you are in your career development. How you establish your personal goals will differ depending upon where you are in your career. That is why goals must be reviewed on a regular basis. And, finally, how you handle success and failure will say a lot about your character development along the way.

What I want to do is look a little closer and deeper into you and your contributions as an employee. I want to talk about the activities in which you will engage. I want to look at the concerns you may be having along the way. I want to explore your motives and your needs as you grow and develop. I want to help you see how your company may be viewing you at the different stages of your career. As I have said, much depends on your experience and your maturity. But, it is with more than just your experience and maturity in mind that I will define those career phases in a more refined manner through **The 5-Phase Career Model**. I want to help you see the meaning of each phase and how you can better understand your own personal development along the way.

As I traveled my own career path, there were times I questioned why I was being given certain assignments or why I was passed over for new positions or why my talents were not being used as I thought they should. Did my managers really understand my background and my talents? Did they not see the potential in my abilities? Why was it taking so long for my talents to be recognized? Or, why didn't my co-workers immediately see the benefits of some of the new ideas and new methods I was bringing forward? After all, I was just out of college and had the latest and greatest training. Or, later, after I had worked on some projects with the accountants or the engineers or the marketers, I was certainly ready to take on greater responsibilities. Why did I need to go through more training? Why was I being trained in areas I was sure I would never use?

How did I not see that I wasn't nearly as ready as I thought I was? Well, it has in part to do with that experience and maturity. We often think we have advanced further in our growth and abilities than we have, most especially early in our careers. Sometimes that self-confidence will outpace our maturity.

It also has to do with how others view us, both our managers and our co-workers. It has to do with the goals that your manager should be helping you to establish. It has to do with the potential that others see in you, as well as your perceived value to the company as a whole. I was fortunate to have some good managers who saw the potential in me and helped me to develop at a good pace. They put me through training to prepare me for future positions. They were guiding me with a foresight that I did not have as a fresh young gun out of college. As I did gain experience and maturity, it all became much clearer for me. That, however, would lead to additional issues as I encountered managers who were not as forward looking or as entrepreneurial as I had become. You can, as I did, begin to enter a transition period where you question with some degree of knowledge how you are, or are not, being directed. It is then that you see the real need for managing your own career. It becomes clear that you are the one ultimately responsible for your professional development. Now, goal setting takes on a whole new meaning for you.

It is near the end of your career when you finally gain all that wisdom that you are able to share with others as you are able to guide them in their career development. It is similar to the time when you realized that your parents were not so dumb after all. You began to have adult conversations with them and discuss adult issues and topics. That is the maturity part of it.

Well, it was with this background that I began to think about how a typical career developed. It was with this in mind that I refined a framework within which you can look at your own career journey. These five phases of career development will help you understand a great deal about your situation at every step of the way. You will have a better understanding of why you might be feeling the way you are at certain points in your career. This understanding will help you to better cope with those feelings. As you understand yourself, it is also important to remember that others are at their own mile-marker on the road of their careers. This can help you better understand how to interact with others.

You will see how your strengths and weaknesses work in your career path. This will help you in setting your goals and expectations. It may also assist you in understanding the expectations that others have of you in various situations. You may better understand why you are getting the assignments and training that you are and see how those assignments and that training will benefit your development in both the near-term and the long-term.

I have defined **The 5-Phase Career Model** based upon your role and your value within the overall business organization over time. Note that I stated *your value within the overall business organization*; I am not talking about your value as a human being. I am only talking about the value that you represent to the business in which you are working as a productive employee. You will see that in looking at your career in this manner, you could be within any of these phases for a varying amount of time based upon your experience and maturity as well as on your personal and professional goals. As an example, if, and when, you change jobs, you may jump into the very first phase again. Your time in this phase will vary depending upon your experience and the needs of the business.

These five phases of a career are fundamental in nature to any career path. The most obvious application of them is with someone at the beginning of their career, basically your first position after completing your training (trade school, college, etc.). You will be able to get the most from understanding these phases. At the same time, however, these phases apply to you should you move to a new position or a new company. For even in those situations, you are starting over to some degree.

So, we will look at how experience, time and your value to the organization affect the phase whether you are just beginning your journey or are simply making a change along the way. A good example, and one we will look at more closely along the way, is the new beginnings that the disciples of Christ were experiencing as they began their new careers after leaving behind their old ones. They were experienced, and maybe some of the best, at their old jobs, but now they were in totally new careers. We will see how they experienced the five career phases in these new careers.

I will also share personal experiences from my own career. While I am not saying that my career was special in some way or that I had some premonition early in my career that led me to a particular understanding, I am saying that my career was not untypical in nature in its overall development. It consisted of successes and failures, highs and lows, and consistency and upheaval. For now, let's take a brief look at the phases of **The 5-Phase Career Model**. A detailed look at each phase will be done in the subsequent chapters.

The Initiation Phase

Your career begins, or perhaps, it begins anew. The Initiation Phase is your beginning in your new job, whether this is your first job following your career training, a new position within your current employer or a new position at a new company. In any case, you are an *initiate* (the noun) in your new role. *Merriam-Webster* defines an initiate as "a person who is being formally accepted or who has been formally accepted as a member of a group or organization."

You were formally accepted as a member of this group which just happens to be your place of employment. You will also be formally accepted, perhaps to varying degrees, by the specific group of people you work with at your place of employment. Now, we don't expect to undergo some initiation ritual as perhaps you may have in joining a sorority or a fraternity. But, there actually are rituals which you will undergo such as meeting with human resources to understand company rules. You will be formally introduced to your co-workers and perhaps to employees in other departments as well. You will undergo the ritual of finding out where you will physically work and obtaining the appropriate tools for your job. There may be rituals with where you park your car. Some spots are simply off-limits for a new employee — and you better be sure to be aware of those spots that are reserved for specific individuals. Depending on your company's culture, you may actually be subject to some type of fun hazing. This is often a test of your personality among your peers. Yes, some businesses will have some fun with your new beginning.

On the other hand, there may be some businesses, or maybe only certain individuals within those businesses, who will test you. They will want to determine how much of a threat you are to them. Are you there to take their job or to take that next promotion that they were planning for? Are you going to try to use the level of your education and flaunt it to your advantage? How far can they go in pushing your buttons until you lose it? There are some people who will want to see you lose it. So, you sort of need to be prepared for whatever comes your way as a new employee.

As this individual who is now a part of a new organization, especially when this is your first job, your role and your activities will likely be well-defined for you. At the same time, you will be finding your way around the business organization as well as learning the culture of the company. Your work will involve you in the basics of your job, and you will continue to be trained, both formally and informally.

Depending upon the position, your experience and the needs of the company, you may be in this phase for as little as 90 days to as long as a year. In some very technical positions, your time may be dictated by your ability to complete specific requirements or certifications. There also could be some overlap with this phase into the next phase. If you should have a longer effective Initiation Phase, then you could be seeing many activities in light of the Integration Phase as well.

The Integration Phase

Let's again take a look at *Merriam-Webster* and see what it has to say about integration. One way the dictionary defines it is as "the combining and coordinating of separate parts or elements into a unified whole." The is about having an understanding of the parts of the business in which you are directly involved. You are beginning to see how the parts of the business fit together in this phase. You are becoming comfortable in working directly with others with a little less hands-on direction by both your co-workers and your supervisor. You have been exploring your situation, and you are now able to define the pieces and see how they coordinate for the benefit of the company. By this time you have learned who some of the go-to people are when you need assistance both within and outside of your own work group. You are gaining a better understanding of the company organization as a whole and where you fit in the big picture.

At this point, you have a good understanding of your own roles and responsibilities; although, they may be still somewhat limited in nature. You are beginning to have an understanding of who you are both personally and professionally. But, you may begin to have some questions about whether or not your abilities are being used to their full potential. You may feel like you should be getting more recognition and more opportunity to display your talents. None of these things are a great concern to you at this time, however.

Your position may be defined generally as that of being skilled, specialty or professional. In a skilled position, you may perform a variety of duties that involve related steps, methods or application of standard practices and specific instructions with occasional variations. You may perform basic research and analysis of information. In a specialty position, you may use advanced and specialized knowledge to perform unique or complex technical tasks or activities. In a professional position, you may use professional concepts and apply company policies and procedures to resolve routine issues. You may perform work that involves various duties with standard processes involving a number of different steps or methods.

The essence of this phase is that you have gained a better understanding of the organization, and you are gaining some limited degree of freedom in your duties while applying standard rules, practices and procedures. And, again, the time you spend in this phase is highly dependent upon your position, your experience and the plans the company has for you. A highly technical position may require much more time as well as additional training. A skilled position that is very methodical in nature may be one that can be quickly learned. You may be in a management training position while also performing your job duties. Your time here may be extended as you may be moved about within your group to gain a broader understanding of the department you are working in.

The Transition Phase

After perhaps some years of time in the first two phases, you enter the Transition Phase. You have probably felt that you should be having more responsibility by now. You may even have strong feelings that you are being underutilized. In a professional position you will be working on tasks of moderate scope where situations require a review and analysis of a variety of factors. You may be to the point of being a seasoned professional with an expert knowledge of some specialty within the company (often referred to as a subject matter expert, or SME). You may be in your first team leader or supervisory role assigning tasks, maintaining schedules and reviewing the work of others. Your managers will be closely evaluating how you handle new responsibilities and how well you are able to take initiative in completing assignments. How you handle difficult situations will be of great interest to your managers.

At this point in your career you are beginning to have a better feel about who you are, what your real gifts and talents are, how to work effectively with others and how to handle those difficult situations. You may have had some promotions, and you likely feel that you are ready for additional responsibilities and promotions. This is a time when you may feel tempted to move on. The grass may seem greener at other opportunities outside of the company. You may feel like you are under-appreciated. You feel like you have made some very good contributions, and you want to be recognized. Perhaps you have been recognized and you want more.

In this phase you should be much more engaged in setting your own goals. You should have a much better understanding of where you want to take your career. Certainly, you see the benefits to be gained in additional experience achieved though a lateral move within or outside the company. This is a concept that may have been difficult to grasp until now as you were only interested in promotions. Up until now you did not see what might be gained through a lateral move.

It is in the Transition Phase that you are finding who you are. It is in this phase that you can see where your possibilities lie within the company. Using the insights you have gained, you feel ready to meet the future.

The Leadership Phase

Having survived the somewhat difficult years of the Transition Phase, you enter the Leadership Phase. As a successful career employee, this is the phase in which you are likely to spend most of your career. This does not necessarily mean that you are in a high-level management position. Yes, it may mean that you are, or it may in that you will be in the future. You could, however, be in a specialty role where you do not manage a single person. You can still be a leader. You may be that person within your own group that others come to for advice and help. You have become that go-to person within your area of responsibility. You may be that person that people come to for the "real" answers when they cannot get them elsewhere. These are the leaders who do not show up as such on the company's organization chart.

But, yes, you may be in a mid- to high-level managerial position, a director position or an executive position. If your aspirations are in management, you will likely pass through various levels at many areas in the organization on your way to higher levels. Broadening your knowledge of the business is a key within your role as a leader, and specifically as a servant-leader.

You are now very much involved in setting more than your own personal goals; you are now engaged in establishing business goals. As part of this you have learned to take calculated risks with an under-standing of risk versus reward. You may be helping others set their goals, and you may be a mentor.

As you near the end of this phase, you know that you are achieving your ultimate business career goals. You have had a clear vision and have followed it. You feel that you have made some good decisions about your career.

The Legacy Phase

You have reached the pinnacle of your career. You have excelled in all areas: communications, leadership, management, planning, fiscal responsibility. You have helped set strategies and vision for yourself and for others. Your thoughts move to life after work. It is not only just about you, however. You want to leave behind a legacy. You want to know you have made a difference. You can see that difference in others you have worked with or mentored. You can see it in the decisions you made along the way. And, now you work to establish a transition plan for someone to move into your position.

You will know when you have reached the Legacy Phase. You will feel it. Age will have something to do with it, but not everything. Some will look forward to an early retirement to live out other dreams, and some will look forward to a late retirement as they fulfill their dreams in their life's work. You will know. It is a good feeling.

Illustrations

On the next several pages I have included three illustrations in graphical format to explain **The 5-Phase Career Model.** Here are some notes regarding these graphs. 1) The X-axis represents Time. This time, however, is not to scale; rather, it is used to represent the relationships of the phases to each other. For example, the graphs show that the Initiation Phase and the Integration Phase are are both relatively shorter in duration than the Transition Phase and Leadership Phase. 2) The Y-axis represents Value. As was previously stated, this is a relative value that the organization has of an employee at any point in their career. For example, you will be of greater value to the organization in the Leadership Phase than you will be in the Initiation Phase. 3) Each phase is separated with a line, but note that the line between the Initiation Phase and the Integration Phase is dotted. This is to represent that there will be some overlap in these phases.

Hopefully, these illustrations help to provide a simple visualization of the five career phases. There is flexibility in the model allowing for variables in one's career goals, direction of the business, career tracks, experience and age. In the remainder of the book, we will look at each phase in detail considering some important aspects of each phase and how to maintain your foundational basics as you manager your career.

Illustration 1

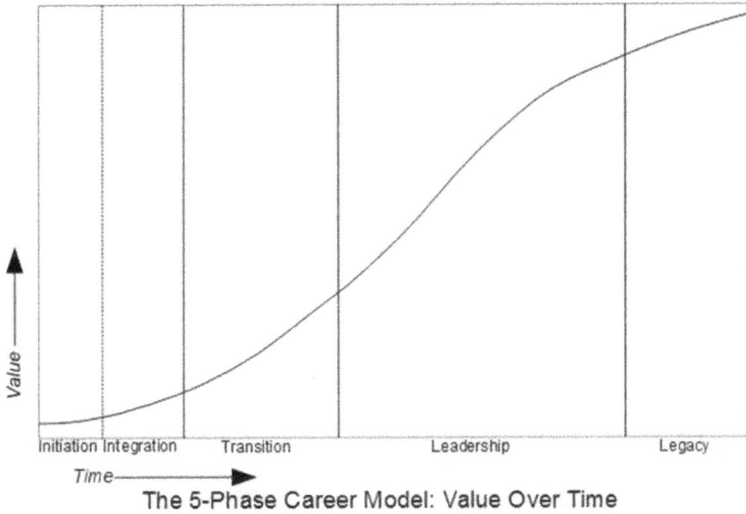

Initiation Integration   Transition   Leadership   Legacy

Time

The 5-Phase Career Model: Value Over Time

Illustration 1 shows what a typical career path might look like. As you progress through time, you pass through each phase. As you pass through the phases, your value to the organization will increase as well. Note that in addition to the Initiation and Integration Phases being relatively short, there will be little increase in your value to the organization during these two phases. The translation of this is that you will not see, and should not expect, large pay increases during this time. Now, note that the Leadership Phase is the longest phase. This is where you will spend the largest amount of time in your career. The type of leadership will be dependent upon your personal career choices and your value to the company. It is in the Leadership Phase that you can expect to see your greatest value, which obviously translates into higher salaries. The typical graph is defined with a slight S-curve, steepest in the Leadership Phase.

Illustration 2

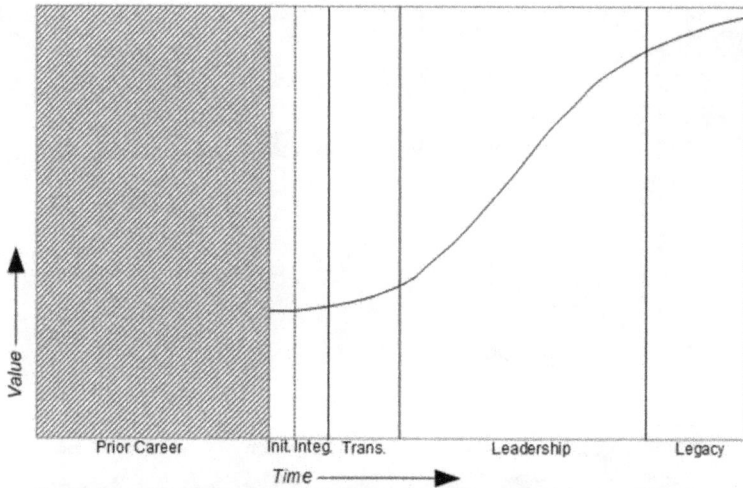

The 5-Phase Career Model: Value Over Time with Career Change

Illustration 2 shows starting over at the Initiation Phase when moving to a new company. The particular move illustrated in this graph could be considered as happening in the Transition Phase. It is not untypical to make a career change at this phase as it could be that time when you are somewhat disillusioned with your career advancement opportunities. So, in this illustration the employee starts at a new company, but the value is obviously higher than that of a first-time new hire. Also note that you are likely to get through the Initiation, Integration and Transition Phases a little faster. This is based on the experience that you have from your previous position. If you are in a position similar to your previous one, the time could be shorter. If you have gone into an entirely new type of business, the time could be longer. Again, the Leadership Phase should be where the greatest amount of your continued career is spent.

Illustration 3

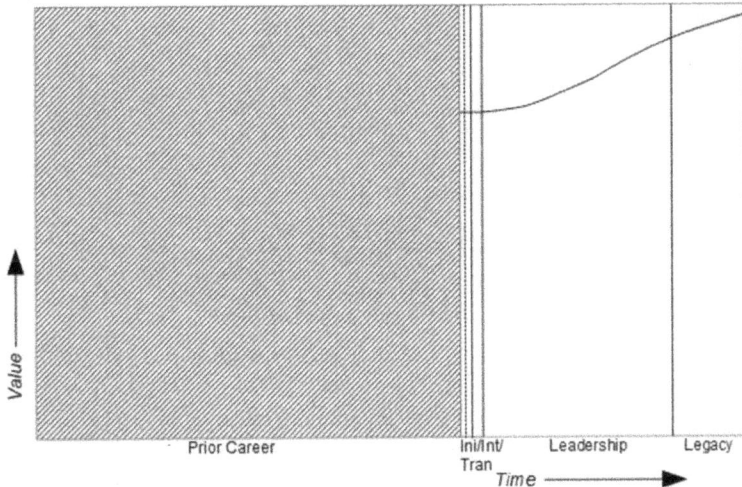

The 5-Phase Career Model: Value Over Time with High-Level Change

Illustration 3 shows a career change at a high organizational level. An example might be of a CEO who leaves one company to become the CEO at another company. This individual's time in the Initiation, Integration and Transition Phases will be relatively short in duration. Obviously, this person is high in value to the new organization. Again, we see the majority of time in the Leadership Phase. This is, of course, dependent upon career goals, experience and age. As with Illustration 2, the S-curve is flatter reflective of the time left in the individual's career from this point.

3

Your Career Begins!
The Initiation Phase

"For I know the plans I have for you," declares the Lord, "plans to prosper you and not to harm you, plans to give you hope and a future" (Jeremiah 29:11 NIV).

The Entry

It is your first day on the job! All your training, education and preparation have paid off. Your parents and/or spouse are proud of you. Shoot, you are proud of yourself. It was tough to get this far. You should feel good. You should have high hopes and expectations. You feel ready and well-prepared. While confident, you may likely feel some bit of nervousness about your first day. The adrenaline may be pumping as you enter the work place. As was stated in the previous chapter, you may spend as much as a year in the Initiation Phase in your career. Perhaps your time in this phase will be dependent upon certain milestones or certifications that must be met. At any rate, while this is not necessarily a lengthy phase of your career, it can be most important. You see, as with any type of new undertaking, say sports for example, there is always room for continuous improvement. You will find this through-out your entire career. But, it is at the beginning, when you are still a rookie, that you will begin to develop lifelong habits. Developing sound personal habits and work habits from the very beginning is so very important. So, we will spend some time discussing what these are and why you need them. They will be important in every phase of your career.

In 2012 LinkedIn began publishing insights from 150 influential leaders. In January 2015, LinkedIn published a series from some of these leaders on their first 90 days in a new job. I checked these out and wanted to share a few thoughts. In his article, Deepak Chopra, M.D., founder of the Chopra Foundation, talked about taking care of yourself. He spoke of applying yourself to the best of your abilities and then going even further. He spoke of taking responsibility for every-thing within your influence. At the same time, he noted that you should not be overwhelmed nor compare yourself with others "to your detriment." He also noted that you should avoid bringing your work home if at all possible. It is good common sense advice. But he went further to say that you have to maintain your personal vision and maintain your health. He wrapped up with nine key points that included avoiding stress, staying active, planning some down time, being honest with yourself and finding a trusted friend you can talk to. This is great advice that you may have trouble following as you are pumped up, ready to prove yourself and very focused.

Inge Geerdens, entrepreneur and founder/CEO of CVWarehouse, shared advice about remaining calm and being patient. She spoke to the importance of listening to others and remaining curious by asking why. You are in a learning situation in your first 90 days and you need to take full advantage of this. You will have a lot of leeway in asking why and seeking explanations. Listen and ask; ask and listen.

Lora Cecere, founder and CEO of Supply Chain Insights, shared this sentiment. She spoke of taking the time to learn the organization and of listening. She noted the importance of listening to what is not said. As a novice in your career, you may tend to feel it is all about you. You need to understand that it is about listening and learning.

Finally, Richard Branson, founder of the Virgin Group, also said, "Simple: listen to everyone you meet." He says that this begins with your first interview which is when you should be asking a lot of questions. He feels the more you can learn about the company in the interview, the farther you will be ahead on your first day. It is also important to find out more about the people you work with which in turn will begin to help you understand the culture. He did caution about not overdoing this to the point of becoming annoying.

I wanted to share these thoughts from these leaders to set a groundwork for some of the habits you should be cultivating from the very start. There will be more about this later. But, as a preview, if there is nothing else you take away, understand the importance of listening. It is a key skill that you must develop and hone. Practice good listening. I will share some ways to do this later.

Now, you may be fortunate enough to have someone who is a mentor to you. This can be valuable in getting to an understanding of the organization in a shorter amount of time. Some companies place selected newly hired employees on a fast-track career path. If that is where you have entered, then you may get additional attention. It is key that you do not let this go to your head! This might be your first lesson in humility. *Clothe yourselves, all of you, with humility toward one another, for God opposes the proud but gives grace to the humble* (1 Peter 5:5 ESV). While being humble means being free from pride and arrogance, it does not mean being weak or passive. When you are humble you do not have to put on a false front. In fact, you will find that in humbleness you will have strength. If you should be confronted, you can speak directly as long as you understand your motives. To be prideful at this phase in your career, or at any phase for that matter, shows others that you care more about yourself than anyone else. Whether as the new person on the team or as a leader, pride and arrogance can quickly destroy any hope of being looked up to. By wanting to look important, you will only make yourself less important. Learn this now, not later.

If you are in some type of fast-track program, there are likely others in such a program as well. In fact, it may be a weeding out process. So, while you may feel good at having been selected and to get the attention, it may be for reasons to thin the crop of new hires. There goes some of that prideful feeling! This is another reason why it is important to be guided by a sound faith-based foundation and the humbleness that it teaches us.

Now — not tomorrow or next week — but now is the time to establish sound work habits. Now is the time to live every aspect of your personal life and your work life with integrity. Now is the time to be reliable and dependable in every situation. Now is the time to perform with quality in every assigned task. Remember, also, now is the time to develop that daily prayer habit. God will listen to the needs you have in your work life as well as your personal life. He doesn't drop you off at the door and tell you to have a nice day without him. He is there for you at all times, but you have some responsibility in this. *When I was a child, I talked like a child, I thought like a child, I reasoned like a child. When I became a man, I put the ways of childhood behind me* (1 Corinthians 13:11 NIV).

The underpinnings of your habits are established on **The Basics** we discussed in **Chapter 1**. We talked about understanding your purpose. This is a lifelong endeavor which will likely change over time. Understanding the influences you have had in your life, and those that you will have going forward, is important to a clear discernment of your life pursuits. Then we looked at **The Ten Critical Foundational Rules** that provide a code of conduct and set societal boundaries for our interaction with others. Finally, we observed how these things lead to basic behaviors and set our foundation of honesty, integrity, ethics, servanthood and chastity.

We will take a look at how this all plays out as you enter your new career in some detail in this Initiation Phase. You are typically in an entry level position. As such you will be following standard practices and procedures while performing straightforward duties. Learning and understanding the standards your company has set for you in your new position is important at this time. While you may see things done in a manner that seems out of step, backward or simply wrong based upon your training and background, it is up to you to learn why the standards are set up as they are. You need to extend some caution with this as you are new and could be perceived as a threat by some. You could be perceived as trying to "upset the apple cart."

Your best approach if you do question some standard practice is to talk to your direct supervisor or manager and obtain clarification. If you should approach another employee, you may not get a proper answer, either because of a misinterpretation on their part or because they see you as a threat and will be cautious about providing you an answer. If at some point in your Initiation Phase you should have a mentor, then they should be a trusted source.

Now, should you be an entrepreneurial type and one who likes to think outside the box, then you may face some push-back as well unless you were placed in a position to utilize those particular abilities. Perhaps you have been assigned to a team whose specific role is to develop new ideas. In that case, move ahead at full speed. If not, then again, bring your ideas to your supervisor or manager or mentor. Get their take on what you are thinking. Be ready to be able to explain your idea well.

When I began my career as a computer programmer, one of the responsibilities that was shirked by many of the programmers was the preparation of documentation. You need to keep in mind that at this time, there was a lot of human intervention in systems processes. The documentation was important for the end-user to properly prepare their input, as well as for the operations personnel to properly prepare that input and process it through multiple steps to the final output. The clearer the documentation, the easier it was for all involved to process information correctly.

Well, the documentation I saw was haphazard and outdated at best in many cases. So, I took it upon myself to develop some basic standards for the preparation of the documentation. I also proposed standards for self-documenting the code. The first part was easy. No one wanted to write documentation. By setting some simple standards, it made it much easier to develop and implement the documentation. I went further and re-wrote the documentation for a number of existing systems. I enjoyed writing and making standards, so this was right up my alley. I took some workload off of the programmers, and this was well-accepted. My standards even became endorsed corporate-wide. All was good. This actually helped me to be more fully accepted by my co-workers.

Now, most programmers have their set way of writing code. So, to attempt to tell them how to change their coding style to make their programs more self-documenting through structured programming was not well-accepted. How dare I, a virtual initiate on their turf, tell them how to write code. Every one of them had much more work experience than I did. I was pushing in a very difficult direction. I was unproven in my abilities as a new employee. This change did not take quick root. I proceeded to use it in my own code, and eventually it was picked up by others when they saw the benefits.

So, I learned you cannot change everything overnight. You can still implement what you can for yourself, but selling it to others may require you to first prove yourself to your work group. With the limited experience that I had this early in my career, the idea that everyone had their own coding style was an issue that was not even on the radar for me. The things you have to watch out for are the things you are not even aware of. Basically, you have to know what you don't know. Now, that is certainly not easy!

Further, had I sold this idea to my manager and had he forced it upon the others, I would have been in an even worse position with my co-workers. What I am saying is that as an initiate, you sometimes have to step lightly. You sometimes have to rein yourself in even when you know you are right. You need to learn when to push hard for your new ideas and when to hold back. This is something that can only be developed as you understand your boundaries through the standards within which you work and understand the team that you are now a part of. Just think of it as part of of your initiation.

Know Your Company

Another big part of your Initiation Phase is learning the company culture. Wherever you did your training, that place had its own culture. Some colleges were known as party schools, some as great sports schools, some as the best business schools and some as the best technical schools. You understood the direction that the school was providing for you, you understood how to prepare your assignments and you understood how to interact with your instructors. You understood something about the culture. You understood what the vision was for you and how you could achieve success.

Well, now you have to understand the vision, mission, values and norms of your new company. You may have done your homework on this prior to interviewing with the company (that is a good idea, by the way). Once within the company, you will find that some of what you were able to learn about the company's culture was marketing hype. Oops, sorry to burst your bubble! Just as you wanted to put your best foot forward on your resume, so does any company on its annual report, web page and other social media. Maybe you were fortunate enough to know someone within the company before you interviewed. This will certainly have provided a much better view of the company culture. In any case, do not be shocked to find that things are not exactly as you expected.

A good way to get a quick understanding about the culture is to ask others in the company to tell you stories about the company. Everyone has a story to share about some unforgettable experience at work. Ask them to share some of these with you. They will likely go a long way in helping you to understand the culture of the business you have entered.

Never be afraid to ask, "Why?" First of all, it is simply a good question to ask. It expresses your interest in the company or the person or the situation at hand. But most importantly, you cannot be afraid to ask questions any time you are unsure. Asking the "why" question is a great way to learn. It will also reveal something about the company culture. Finding out the ultimate reason for why a particular action is taken or why something is performed in some particular manner can be very revealing. Answers like, "Because we've always done it that way," or "Because the boss said to do it that way," reveal one thing. Answers like, "Because we completed a recent study which revealed …," or "Because it saves time and money," reveal quite another view of how your company operates within certain cultural values.

Ask the "why" questions and pay attention to the answers. Similar answers over time from various sources will be insightful about the company culture.

Know Yourself

If you have not done so, now is the time to establish your career goals for the next year. Where do you want to be at the end of your first year? What do you want to be doing? What do you want to have achieved? How do you want to be perceived in the workplace? What additional training do you feel you need? Ask yourself why you see yourself in the position you do after your first year. How are you going to get there?

From the questions asked, you can see that one thing setting goals does for us is to keep us moving. Sometimes you may have a difficult day. You wonder what you are doing and where you are going. That is a good time to pull out your goals and remind yourself of where you are going and what you are doing. Keep in mind that you also have personal goals, and sometimes your personal goals and your career goals are very much entwined. Goals can be established to let you take big steps or small steps, but without any goals your steps are aimless wandering.

Setting goals also helps to build your character. It may take many years for you to realize that it is not necessarily the accomplishment of your goals that has made you what you are. More often it is what has happened along the way that built your character. Remember the adage, "It's the journey, not the destination." Yes, we want to and need to get to the end to achieve our goal. But, oftentimes, it is how we got there, how we achieved our goal, that makes the difference and builds our character. Did you take the easy way rather than accepting a more challenging opportunity that allowed you to learn and to grow? Did you develop your honesty and integrity in the achievement of your goals? Did you enhance your skills along the way?

Goals can also be a statement of faith. You are going to be given goals that seem unattainable. These are often referred to as "stretch goals." They are designed as stated, to stretch your abilities and help you to grow. So, maybe you accept these with a bit of faith asking for a higher form of assistance in reaching those goals. For remember, God wants to help us be successful in all areas of our lives.

You certainly like to be rewarded. Good goals allow that to happen. The reward might be as simple as a thanks, or it might lead to a bonus or a promotion. And sometimes, the reward is that wonderful feeling inside of a job well done.

In all likelihood, you will sit down with your supervisor and prepare work objectives for the year. This is a great start. In fact, you may be asked to prepare your personal goals. At the end of the first year, you will sit down again for a final evaluation of how well you met your objectives. Hopefully, and assuming you have a quality leader, the end of the year will not be your only feedback. You should be receiving regular feedback throughout the year. Deciding where your career will be at the end of your first year should not be difficult.

But now, think about a career plan for five years out. Maybe you thought you could be running a department by the end of five years. Perhaps you wanted to simply be the best _____ (fill in the position or title) you could be by this time. Maybe you had already planned to get a couple of years of experience with this company and move on to bigger things. The plan is yours. And, this plan is not set in concrete; it will change as you grow to understand yourself and as you gain experience. There are also going to be many unexpected bumps in the road along the way that will totally change your direction. For now, it is about establishing that ideal for yourself so you have a target. There are plenty of good books on setting career goals. You can also likely get help from your manager and your human resources department. Yes, this will require you to do some homework. This does not need to be anything extravagant. It will also be something that, for some of you, will not be easy to accomplish. Do the work and don't delay.

Here is one other thing you can give some thought to at this time. This may be even more difficult. This is your own personal vision and values. Your company has a vision and values statement, why not develop one for yourself? The reason this may not be easy at this time is that you are still getting to know yourself. You think you know what you want to be and may have some idea of how to get there, but can you place this in a vision and values statement? How well do you really know yourself? This exercise will require some quiet time and some real soul-searching.

About halfway through my career (so, obviously not in the Initiation Phase), I developed a personal vision and values statement. That was in 1992. I have this on my desk as I am writing this, and every bit of it is just as relevant today as it was 23 years ago. In reviewing this statement, I find it will serve me for the reminder of my life. You see, if you take the time to understand who you are and who you are in Christ, it can guide you well for a very long time. At this stage of your life, you may or may not be ready to develop your personal vision and values. And if you do, they may not stand for 23 years. You may have to update them as you mature and gain a better understanding of yourself. Be honest with yourself. If you do not understand enough about yourself, then maybe a better understanding of you is part of your vision and values statement. It is a nice exercise that you will want to re-evaluate from time-to-time. I have included my own **Personal Vision and Values** in **Appendix 4** along with a little explanation that may assist you in preparing yours.

You Are Not Prepared

You may take an affront to the statement in this section heading, and I cannot say that I blame you. However, even in the most technical position, you are not prepared for your job. Your training has provided a good foundation upon which to build. You must keep in mind that your chosen industry has peculiarities that are unique to that industry. And further, the company you have gone to work for will have its own ways of doing business that are even more varied.

When I started my career in the telecommunications industry, I found that their accounting structure was totally different than standard accounting practices. I had taken basic accounting classes at the university, so I did understand the essentials. But as strange as it may seem, debits and credits were handled in the opposite manner that they were in every other industry. I never found out the reason for this, and, frankly, I did not care. All I knew was that as a computer programmer, it was really important that I understood this.

In another example, way back when I began my career, the details of phone calls were recorded on punched paper tape. Yes, that is correct, not magnetic tapes or disks, but on paper! I sure was not taught in school how to handle input from a paper tape source. I had not even heard of such a thing. So, I had to learn how to read the punched holes in those spools of paper tape as I worked on debugging the programs that processed them. And, the punched code was an entirely new form of code to me. As I became the lead programmer for our toll processing and billing systems, I became so familiar with the punched paper tape code that I could pull the paper tape through my hands and read it with my fingers at a rather fast rate. Yes, your company will have its own uniqueness as well.

You are in a continuous state of learning. You must be open to this. Don't think that your degree or your certification or your focused technical training has made you fully prepared for your initial entry into the workforce. Your training has done two things for you as you enter your first job. First of all, you have proven that you have some degree of knowledge in your selected field. You have shown that you have the ability to learn. This also means you have some degree of skills in organization and planning to have completed your studies in whatever format they have taken.

Here's an interesting note concerning one of my early job interviews. I interviewed for a programmer position with Sears in Chicago. I was pleased to have been selected following a preliminary interview on campus. The qualities they were looking for in prospective employees were their achievements with regard to grades and with regard to extracurricular activities. I fulfilled both requirements as a high-performing student athlete. When I arrived at the interview there was a room filled with potential candidates for the position. Now, there were multiple positions open, but I did not know how many. I found out in talking with some of the other candidates that they were not all computer science majors. In the interview I learned that Sears was looking for a potential in employees beyond coding skills. They were truly after people who were intelligent learners and had quality interactive skills and communications skills. They felt that coding skills could be learned by quality employees who had other skills necessary to succeed in the business world. From the outset, continuous learning was an expectation.

The second thing your training has provided for you is an open door. You have met minimum requirements to be considered for your position. The training you have obtained in your chosen field of study has provided you a way to be considered for a position, and eventually to be hired. It has not necessarily provided you with all of the skills you are going to need on your first day, or on some day five or ten years from now. You are not fully prepared on the first day which is why you will go through an Initiation Phase. And, what you will be doing in the next five or ten years will likely be very different than what you may be imagining at this point. You simply must be in a continuous state of learning for all of your career. This will be in both formal and informal settings as you progress through your career.

Listen!

As you learn to know your new work group and strive to get a handle on standard operating practices for your position, you will next step outside of your work group to understand the roles and responsibilities of other employees and other departments outside of your work group. You will begin to learn how your team does business, perhaps both within and outside the company depending upon your role. In my role as a programmer, this came rather early in my Initiation Phase as it was part of the position to develop and support other departments. Within your own set of responsibilities you will be supporting someone else in some way.

A critical trait in this area is communications. In fact, this is one of the most important aspects that you should practice and practice and practice. Good communications skills will be vital for your entire career; they are crucial in developing your career to its fullest potential. Various research shows that as much as 80% of one's professional time is spent communicating. Of that number, 30% of the time is spent speaking, and 45% of the time is spent listening (Adler 2001). The key take-away at this point is that while communicating is a two-way street, most of your time should be spent listening. Especially in this phase of your career, you should be listening much more than you are talking. That 45% figure should be much higher early in your career, perhaps 60%-70%.

I have some notes from a study I read in the early 2000s (unfortunately I have been unable to locate the source) that says that the time one spends practicing and evaluating their own communications skills is in the range of 0%-2%, most of it at the lower end. The study further noted that our career success or failure depends to an extraordinary degree on communications excellence. I would totally agree with the second statement. You do have plenty of opportunity to practice your communications skills on a daily basis. Simply be clear, concise and courteous on every phone call and in every face-to-face communication. Next, spell check everything you write. Nothing stands out as sloppy and as careless as misspelling, except for perhaps sloppy English (although there seems to be somewhat of a dumbing down, in my view, of the use of proper English). Use people's names in conversation, both at work and outside the workplace. Smile when you speak to someone. Show your interest by looking at them when they are talking.

You will be receiving a lot of information in this early phase of your career. You will be getting information from your human resources department, likely undergoing training that is specific to your business. As previously mentioned, you will be learning the standard operating procedures for the work in which you are engaged. You will be learning about the corporate organization chart and how the pieces fit together. The amount of information coming at you will be voluminous and important. While numbers have been tossed around about how much we retain, some more recent studies show that people forget at widely different rates based on a number of factors. Obviously, the more complex, unfamiliar or uninteresting the information is, the more difficult it will be to recall. The point to be made is that good listening is a key to recall (Thalheimer 2010).

In the Initiation Phase, there are some areas of particular importance with regard to listening. While these are important throughout your career, now is the time to get them right and establish those good habits. While not an exhaustive list, let's take a look at some of the reasons you will want to establish good listening skills:

- **Get the directions for your assignment right**. This sounds pretty basic. You do not want to take off on your first project in the wrong direction. And — this is critical — if you did miss something or you are unsure about what you heard, then ask for clarification. Believe me, you are far better off asking now than finding out farther down the road that you took the wrong direction. No one will fault you for asking a question. On the other hand, performing the assignment incorrectly will have consequences.

- **Get the timeline for an assignment correct**. This is related to the first point, but it is of its own importance. If you have not clarified this, the results can be disastrous, or at best extremely embarrassing. You may have all the specifications correct and understand the overall goal of the project. But if you have spent some degree of time on the project and you are suddenly asked why you have not finished, you will have that blank-faced stare on your face. If others are depending upon you to have completed your portion of a larger project on time, then you have affected more than just yourself by not listening well. If unsure, then ask. Here is one thing you may as well learn right now: there are no dumb questions. Clarify until you have no doubts. This will save you a world of heartache.

- **Get the specifications that your client is asking for correct**. Your assignment may involve you working with others outside of your area. You may be told to get the details from someone else. First of all, make sure you know who you are to get the specifications from. The wrong source could mean that you have the wrong information. Should you ask the wrong person, they may not want to appear to be uninformed and could thus steer you in the wrong direction. This very issue was discussed previously in the **Basic Behaviors** section in **Chapter 1**. You should know it is okay to say, "I don't know." Can you rely that others feel the same? Or, as was warned, are they only concerned about saving face or looking good? If you must get direction from others, then be sure you have listened so that you do go to the right source.

- **Remember someone's name after a first introduction**. The most important words that anyone can hear is their own name. Remember it correctly, or ask! Unfortunately, I have always had a problem with names. I was managing a data center, and auditors were visiting from our corporate office. Being aware of my problem remembering names, I did some reading on how to do better with this. I studied and practiced. The lead auditor walked into my office and introduced herself. I was trying to go over in my mind the best way to recall her name. We sat and talked for about a half-hour on how they would proceed with the audit. We then walked out of my office and stopped at the desk of one of my supervisors. I introduced the lead auditor but completely went blank on her name. What could I do? I politely asked her once again for her name as I introduced her. While I was totally embarrassed, I tried not to show it. I would like to say I have worked hard and improved in this area, but, alas, I have not. All I can say is get this one right early and practice it often.

- **Understand someone else's side of an argument**. This is not always easy to do, especially if you let your ego get in the way. If you are going to be able to defend your position, you must completely understand the other person's position. If you are only willing to hear what you want to hear, you will have real trouble winning them over as they will see that you are simply not listening to what they have to say. They will likely end up walking away and blowing you off.

- **Get opinions and facts before making a decision**. Know the difference. It is easy to get caught up in our own thoughts and habits and processes. We have to be careful in being blind to the facts. Approach the situation with an open mind. An open mind does not mean you have surrendered your opinions, it merely means you are willing to listen. You must listen carefully to understand facts and opinions. You must also understand your own thoughts and know your own facts from opinions.

Here are a few thoughts that may help with listening:

- **When listening to another, give them your full attention.** Show a real interest in what the other person is sharing. Look at them. Look in their eyes. This takes real effort on your part. Do not try to fake this!
- **Take notes.** Since retention of information drops off rapidly, especially technical and unfamiliar information, taking notes will ensure you have the information at hand for later reference.
- **Repeat what you have heard to show the other person that you understand.** This is an extremely good method for assuring you have the correct information. This is easy enough to put into practice.
- **Ask questions.** If the individual has said something that is unclear, then ask. Remember, no dumb questions!
- **Read body language.** Watch the person's facial expressions and eyes. See how they stand. When I managed a team all of whom were remote to my location, reading body language was not an option. You have to learn to use the same concept in a different manner. In weekly staff meeting conference calls, I would listen for tones in someone's voice to understand how they were feeling about what they were saying. This does take some time as you learn to know each individual, but even with individuals you do not know, some clues are unmistakable. A rise in volume is easy enough to detect as is a sigh or a laugh or a momentary silence. Look for clues in email correspondence. Sometimes the very volume of the email could indicate the degree of importance to the sender. At the same time, a short curt note could have another meaning. The degree of formality or informality can also be an indicator.

Listening takes a lot of work. It is an important trait to develop.

Good listeners are recognized as being open and approachable. Good listeners display an interest (that cannot be faked!) in others that they will find comforting. They will sense a fairness in you. And when you disagree with them, they will know that you have at least given them a fair chance to make their case.

Beyond listening for the good of others, remember that the key reason for listening is to get the facts and understand the situation. In order to make a truly informed decision or take a calculated risk, you must listen. *To answer before listening — that is folly and shame* (Proverbs 18:13 NIV).

Organize for Productivity

If you have been a disorganized individual, now is the time to begin new habits. If you are already well-organized, perhaps you can look at new or different processes. Being organized means more than just having your most used apps easily accessible on your latest version of the iPhone®. No, it means organizing your work space, your calendar and your to-do list. It is how you handle your email, phone calls, meetings, files and assignments. Most often you will hear the term time management used when discussing the organization of your work activities. Unfortunately, you cannot stop and start time. You cannot manage time, but you can manage how you utilize the time that you have been given.

In an article from the *Harvard Business Review* on-line, productivity expert Jordan Cohen is quoted as saying that it is really all about productivity. "We have to get away from labeling it 'time management.' It's not about time *per se* but about how productive you can be" (Gallo 2014). Let's face it, however, in the Initiation Phase of your career, and especially in the first weeks and months, you may not have a lot of control over managing your productivity. In fact, you might well be engaged in some type of structured training program. This does not mean, though, that you should not develop a system.

There are plenty of good books and websites on this topic. If you do not have a plan, do some work to find one. Ask your manager or your mentor or co-workers for suggestions. The business, or perhaps your department or division, may well have standard tools that you will be expected to use. It is also important to keep in mind that what works for others may not be as effective for you. I personally took advantage of quite a number of different tools throughout my career. There are many very good digital tools. But, I often found myself reverting back to a paper planning calendar (it was typically a Day-Timer®). It was just much easier for me when I needed to check open schedules within either the near-term or the long-term. It was small enough to carry to meetings as well as to leave open on my desk for easy access. While this worked well for me, there was a lot of trial and error for me to figure this out. It may take some time to discover what works best for you.

Now, as I was saying, in this very early phase of your career, your control over your plans may be limited to some extent. As I began my career as a programmer I was also placed on a fast-track management training program. Many of my early weeks and months were spent outside of my own work area. I kept a paper notebook with me at all times to take notes, clarify assignments and track my schedule. Sometimes simpler is better.

No matter your degree of control over your schedule, there are several items that can and should be given consideration with regard to organization and productivity:

- **Set goals and milestones**. When you are assigned a task, you should be provided with a time for completion. If you have not been provided with a due date, then ask! There are no open-ended tasks. Your tasks are sure to involve some steps that lead to completion. Work backwards from the due date to establish milestones for yourself for completion of each step or phase of your project. This will not only keep you on track, but when your manager asks for a status update, you will be able to respond in a meaningful way about your progress.
- **Keep a prioritized to-do list**. This should be a simple, easily

updated and manageable list. Prioritizing items is a must. Without assigning proper priorities it is too enticing to work on the easiest items or on the items that make you appear to be busiest. No, you must work on the most important tasks first. I will admit, there were times when I ignored this rule. If I was stumped on a project, if I was waiting on more information, or if I simply had a mental block, I might pull out one of those easy tasks. Sometimes a quick hit on an easy task was just what was needed to free my mind. Just be cautious about over-doing this type of thing.

- **Keep one calendar**. Whether it is an electronic calendar, an app your work group uses, or a paper-based calendar, keep just one. Trying to maintain multiple calendars is too time consuming. It can also lead to errors when trying to keep multiple calendars from varying medias or sources in sync.

- **Schedule your time**. Again, as a new employee and depending on your position, you may have much of your time scheduled for you. You do, of course, need to include all of those items on your calendar. But for that time in your day over which you do have control, schedule your time wisely. Schedule time during the day to check and respond to email. You can also schedule time to respond to phone calls. If you need some support from other sources, schedule time with those sources to ensure you have the appropriate amount of time to discuss your needs. It is also common courtesy to coordinate with those individuals and not just pop in and interrupt their day. After all, others schedule their time as well.

- **Do it right the first time**. If you rush to complete a task early but it has errors or is actually incomplete because your were hurrying, you have only lost time that had been devoted to this project. You now have to answer for your errors or mistakes as well as re-do the work. You have now taken more time from the person you did the work for. They reviewed it once. Now, they will review it a second time, and this time much more closely. And, they will likely be more apt to look at your next results for your next project more closely as well. Quality work is important; it is more important than beating a deadline. Re-work is a waste of your productive time. Do it right the first time. (Did I repeat myself? I sure did!)

- **Handle it now**. This is especially important in dealing with your emails. Don't let unanswered emails pile up or think that you have taken care of them by putting them in a holding folder. This may sound somewhat counterproductive at first as these will often be interruptions. The key is in how you handle it. First of all, you do not need to let every email interrupt your work. Set aside certain times during the day to check your emails. If you do not do this, you will spend way too much time being interrupted as you try to concentrate on the work in front of you. This similarly applies to phone interruptions with a couple key exceptions: 1) a call from your boss likely should be answered, and 2) if you are waiting on someone to return a call, then you should respond; there is nothing worse than playing phone tag. Also keep in mind that in your early phase, your manager may want things handled in a specific manner. You should obviously honor her requirements.

  Next, there are basically four ways to respond whether you are taking action now or taking action at a later time that you have set aside for this activity. One, you can handle whatever it is immediately. For example, if you are waiting for information, then get it and act on it. Two, add the item to your to-do list; don't forget to prioritize it! Three, delete the item. If it was of no importance, then eliminate it immediately. Four, while this may not be available to you in the early phase of your career, delegate the item to someone else.

- **Don't put off difficult tasks**. You may fear difficult tasks at this point in your career for any number of reasons. You may be unsure about your ability to accomplish the assignment. It might stretch your abilities beyond your current knowledge base. You may feel you might end up looking stupid. You may simply fear failure. Whatever the issue, the best way to handle difficult tasks is head-on at full steam. This does not mean you jump in haphazardly. It means doing the hard work. It may require additional research. You may have to go back for clarification a second or third time. This is okay. Getting you outside of your comfort zone is not uncommon for you in this Initiation Phase. Your management wants to see how well you can handle a bit of stress.

- **First things first, and wrong things never.** First things first means spending time on the high-priority items from your list of assignments. Be sure you are providing the service you are being paid to provide. There is absolutely no time in your day to do the wrong things. What do I mean? Here is the best example. You have a bit of time on your hands as you await a phone call. So, you jump on the internet to check on something personal —an order, Facebook, week-end plans, a humorous video someone told you about. The internet presents a literal world of information at your fingertips. It is way too easy to spend too much personal time on the internet. Even if your company allows it, I say you should avoid it. It is completely non-productive time. In effect you are robbing your company or your client in doing this.

   I am retired, and the only person I rob in my personal time on the internet is me. I still don't like it. I take a little time each morning before I begin my exercise program to check emails and some websites that I follow. Almost without exception, I spend at least a half-hour more time than I planned for this activity. I know you cannot speed up time, but it sure seems as such when you start reading and searching and following links on the internet. Stay off the internet for any personal use at work; this is a time robber! Rob yourself if you must, but do not rob your company or your customers.

If you really, honestly have some free time, then work on a low-priority item, engage in some self-training, clean your work area, clear your emails and phone calls, make a list of areas where you need more knowledge, review your personal goals, think of something entrepreneurial, or learn something new about your company, your customers or your co-workers. There are plenty of opportunities for you to fill your "free" time.

- **Keep your desk or your work space clean and uncluttered**. When you need something, you don't want to waste your time searching through clutter, especially if your boss is standing over you while you search. When you have finished with something, put it away. I always found it was productive to take some time after the end of the work day just to clean-up my work area and prepare for the next day. Some people prefer to do something similar by coming in early before the work day begins. I found that when I came in early to get organized, I was ready to go to work. Organizing fell immediately out of my scope. So, end-of-day clean-up was always best for me.

But be sure that everything is done properly and in order (1 Corinthians 14:40 NLT). The writer was speaking about a worship service being conducted in an orderly manner. Good organization has been recognized since the earliest times of organized society.

Good Habits

How do you start out Day One on the job? Did you polish your shoes? Do you have on a nice new shirt or blouse? Did you eat a good breakfast like your mom always told you? Have you allowed enough time so you won't be late on your first day?! (Come on, you know being late is not acceptable!)

There is that one most important thing for Day One: prayer. If you do not have a habit of daily prayer, why not use your Day One as the day to begin? You are starting a new life, a new career. In effect, you are no longer that individual who just the day before was a graduate of some education or training process. Today, you are a different person. Now is a most opportune time to really make your life new by beginning with daily prayer. It is one habit to begin now if you are not already doing so. Do not wait until tomorrow! Now is the time to begin this new habit.

Spend some time with the one who has guided you to this point. Show your thanks to him. Maybe you didn't get your ideal job or the job you really wanted. That doesn't matter. You are changing and growing. It is a time for thanks.

And, maybe you have the Day One jitters. What better way to settle yourself than by spending some quiet time with God. He'd love to talk with you. It doesn't have to be some long drawn out prayer. It doesn't have to be some memorized verse. How about just acknowledging his presence in your life? How about saying thanks for all he has blessed you with? How about asking for help in settling in on Day One? How about simply listening for any guidance you may be seeking? It cannot be emphasized more how important it is to develop a daily habit of talking quietly with God. Do not wait. If you have not already developed a daily prayer habit, begin it on Day One. It is a life-long habit that will serve you well.

And, remember, you should be humble. When I started at my new job out of college, I was pretty excited to get started. To some degree, I had to curb this enthusiasm. You see, as I found out after a short time, I was the first college graduate in the IT department. People were a little wary of me, especially my co-workers. Perhaps I was seen as a smart-ass college kid who was there to throw my degree around. Fortunately, that was not my style. I did play nice with others. In fact, I was early humbled by what I did not know. As I added to the value of the group with some of my strengths, I did so quietly and did not try to take credit.

Listen to advice you received before you even started school. You should have learned very early in life to say "please" and "thank-you." You are not now, nor will you ever be, above using those words frequently. Proverbs 22:6 (NIV) tells us, *Start children off on the way they should go, and even when they are old they will not turn from it.* Yep, we learned it as children, and we should practice it all our lives. And, of course, there is the "Golden Rule," *So in everything, do to others what you would have them do to you, for this sums up the Law and the Prophets* (Matthew 7:12 NIV). "Please" and "thank-you" should be a large part of our vocabulary. It gets back to being humble. You are not above asking kindly and accepting graciously. If you want to grow as a servant-leader, you have to understand **The Basics (Chapter 1).**

There will come the day not long after you begin your job when you will receive your first paycheck. That is one of the best feelings ever. You are likely filled with excitement. Have you thought about what you are going to do with your first paycheck? Some may already be planned to pay off loans. There are groceries, clothes for work, maybe some furnishings. If you have a family, then there are many, many other considerations. You probably at least want to have some bit of fun with your first paycheck, maybe a nice meal out. These are all good things, deserved things.

But, have you thought about the first things? We should honor God by voluntarily returning some of the blessings he has provided for us. When it comes to money, the real question is, is our heart in the right place? Are we putting our money where our heart is? We can tell where our heart is by seeing where we are putting our money. *For where your treasure is, there your heart will be also* (Matthew 6:21 NIV).

Christians have received the riches of God's grace and are to respond with generosity and giving. Followers of the way of Christ are called to a life of service, sharing and stewardship. We have an obligation to do good. The old covenant required simple percentages for tithing. Everyone knew how much was required. The new covenant has no set percentages. Instead, it requires more soul-searching, more training for the conscience, more selfless love for others, more faith, more voluntary sacrifice and less compulsion. It tests our values, what we treasure most, and where our hearts are. Your church is certainly not the only place to be giving. There are other causes that you may personally want to support with your treasure. That is fine. Many charitable organizations run on shoe-string budgets and are constantly in need of support. Also, remember that this support can also be in terms of time. Using your talents and giving your time for the needs of others is also a faithful way to give. Now is the time to start your good habit of giving back.

This is a decision that you may not be making alone if you have a spouse and a family. It is something you need to openly communicate about. For some, this will be simple and easy, for others it will be a struggle when you look at all the bills.

The Disciples

Some are going to question why I am looking at the disciples of Jesus when giving instruction on career management. That is certainly a fair question. If you are not a believer in the divinity of Christ, but you are still reading at this point, then keep an open mind. While you may not believe in his divinity, you cannot dismiss his influence throughout the world for the last 2000 years, as well as the fact that there is some really good advice for living your life in the books inspired by his life. Those who were first to be influenced by his teachings were a group who followed him, became his disciples and then gave up their personal careers to set upon a new path with him. We will see how their new careers developed with regard to **The 5-Phase Career Model**.

The word disciple is derived from the Greek word which means learner, or student. There were many who followed Jesus and listened to his teachings. We see throughout the gospels that there were thousands who were drawn to listen to him, to follow him. Some of those became his students, disciples who were eager to learn of the ways of his teachings in greater detail. We see at one point, in fact, in Luke 10 that he sent seventy-two disciples (seventy in some translations) ahead of him to all the towns he intended to visit. He gave them specific instructions about how to act and what to say. When they returned, they were joyous about what they had accomplished as students. So, there were a very great number of followers, and some lesser number of actual students.

Of course, we hear mostly of the twelve disciples who were closest to Jesus. They became his inner circle of students. They would get very close hands-on immersive learning with Jesus as they traveled from town to town. These twelve are specifically named for us in the Gospels, but other disciples are also named in the Gospels. These others include: Cleopas, James (the brother of Jesus), Joanna, Joseph of Arimathea, Joseph Barsabbas, Judas/Jude (the brother of Jesus), Lazarus, Mary (the mother of James and Joseph), Mary of Bethany, Mary Magdalene, Matthias (who replaced Judas Iscariot), Salome and Susanna (RW Research 2004). While there were numerous disciples, or learners, Jesus was looking for those few who would form a close-knit group. He had special plans for them. Maybe kind of like that fast-track management training program you are on as an initiate in your company. Of course, their work would result in a far different outcome than yours.

They all had some type of career prior to becoming followers and then students of Jesus. So, they were starting entirely new careers as initiates in a job that they had never expected to be in. And, this can happen in your own career as circumstances dictate. Well, I want to take a look at how their new careers progressed relative to The 5-Phase Career Model. After all, we are talking about the gifted way to manage your career, and it was these twelve disciples who experienced the gift first hand.

Obviously, they were not entering their new careers as first-time workers. They all had existing jobs that they left to pursue a new following. That is certainly not uncommon in our own careers. Some people make very drastic career changes just as these twelve did. So, we will look at them in each career phase along the way.

First, a little background. We generally tend to think of these twelve disciples as a very diverse group, and they were. But, as we will see, some of them actually had quite a bit in common.

There was some prior knowledge of Jesus for some of them. John and James (son of Zebedee) were cousins of Jesus. Additionally, James (son of Alphaeus) and Matthew may have been brothers and also cousins of Jesus. While brothers, Matthew and James were likely very different. As a tax collector, Matthew likely had some education and was fluent in Aramaic, Greek and Latin. In his position as a servant to the Roman rulers, he was scorned by the Jews. A patriotic and idealistic nationalist, James would have been at total odds with his brother (McBirnie 2004, pp. 138-140).

Other brothers in the group include Andrew and Simon Peter. They were fishermen in partnership with John and James (son of Zebedee). Thaddaeus/Jude was the son of James (son of Zebedee) and also involved in the fishing business. Finally, Thomas may have known John since childhood (McBirnie 2004, p. 116).

Simon the Zealot may not have been the only member of the extreme and violent Jewish nationalist party that sought to drive out the Romans. Some traditions hold that possibly James (son of Alphaeus) and Thaddeus/Jude may also have been Zealots. According to this tradition, James was put off by the bloodshed of the Zealots and left to become an ascetic (RW Research 2004 and McBirnie 2004, p138-139).

A number of the twelve disciples had also been followers of John the Baptist. This includes Simon Peter, Andrew, Philip, Bartholomew/Nathanael, and possibly Thomas, James (son of Zebedee), James (son of Alphaeus) and Thaddaeus/Jude. It seems quite possible that all twelve had been followers of John the Baptist (Bruce 1871). Andrew had even been assisting John in baptizing others according to some traditions (McBirnie 2004, p. 49). It seems safe to say that they were all spiritually earnest men.

All but one of the twelve, that being Judas Iscariot, were from and/or lived in the same area of Galilee. For those leaving their way of life to follow Jesus, we see them dropping everything at a moment's notice. Perhaps, however, they had been well-prepared and full of expectation by John's preaching. At any rate, they left their current jobs for new careers (Bruce 1871).

In his book *The Training of the Twelve*, author Alexander B. Bruce paints a nice picture of the training of the twelve disciples. He notes that while they may have been earnest in their spirituality, they were by no means mature in their faith. They were happy to be in the presence of the one whom John the Baptist had prepared the way for, but they still had a deeper maturity to establish in their newly developing careers. This is just what you see as you enter the Initiation Phase of your own career. Of course, you are not really aware of your lack of maturity; rather, it is something that will be clear once you have achieved a greater degree of maturity.

Bruce discusses three stages in the development of the disciples. In the first stage, they are "simply believers in him as the Christ, and his occasional companions at convenient, particularly festive, seasons." He talks of a second stage when "fellowship with Christ assumed the form of an uninterrupted attendance on his person, involving entire, or at least habitual abandonment of secular occupations." Early on, many of them continued to work at their prior jobs, especially the fishermen, as evidenced by their activities in the Gospels. Many also had their families with them when they were following Jesus. But, more and more they were becoming all-in with Jesus.

Finally, Bruce talks of a third stage when "they were chosen by their Master from the mass of his followers, and formed into a select band, to be trained for the great work ..." We will see as we go through each of the five phases of career development how these men grew and matured and transformed into the leaders that Christ had prepared them to be so that they could carry on his works after he departed.

Jesus was looking not only for disciples to follow him, but also for disciples who could eventually make disciples of others. He planned a careful, painstaking education for them so that Jesus' influence in the world would be permanent.

Bruce lists the qualifications for the disciples as spirituality, freedom from narrow-minded thinking, sympathy towards all people, dignity, willing to bear the cross, freedom of conscience, a large heart and an enlightened mind. However, the ones Jesus called were "ignorant, narrow-minded, superstitious, full of Jewish prejudices, misconceptions and animosities. They were men of humble birth, low station, mean occupations, uneducated, little interaction with cultivated minds." Wow, quite a mismatch! Jesus, however, saw into the hearts of these men and saw their spiritual fitness. Nothing else in their pasts mattered to him. He knew what he could make of these men. He saw that those who deemed themselves better than these men were too proud to be disciples.

Now, each of you is not likely that mismatched to your new position, but you are likely not as well-fit as you think. And, remember, you have to get **The Basics (Chapter 1)** right!

Let's take a look at Jesus' followers, the disciples, as they began their careers working for Jesus. They came from various walks of life as they entered into Jesus' ministry. Their background was with life experience according to their particular roles at the time they gave it all up to follow Jesus. So, they were certainly initiates in this ministry. They had a lot to learn about their roles and the new business venture with this man named Jesus. One key for them is that they were called to their new roles. Perhaps you have felt similarly about your new role. Sometimes we feel as if we were drawn to this point in time through powers greater than our own. And sometimes, it just feels like a job. However you are feeling, just remember that one greater than you is in control!

The disciples were pulled from whatever work they were performing, work that had somehow prepared them for their journey with Jesus, into a new group. They each became a member of this new group, they were initiates. Thus, as they began their new jobs, they had much to learn. Surely, Jesus considered their background experience, their previous immersive learning, if you will. For example, we read in

Matthew, *Now as Jesus was walking by the Sea of Galilee, He saw two brothers, Simon who was called Peter, and Andrew his brother, casting a net into the sea; for they were fishermen. And He said to them, "Follow Me, and I will make you fishers of men." Immediately they left their nets and followed Him. Going on from there He saw two other brothers, James the son of Zebedee, and John his brother, in the boat with Zebedee their father, mending their nets; and He called them. Immediately they left the boat and their father, and followed Him* (Matthew 4:18-22 NASB).

We see that Jesus will use their prior training and experience as a beginning and grow their abilities through his training. They will need to learn more about their leader and his way. They were just beginning their (new) careers.

Entering this Initiation Phase, you have a base of training and experience. As we saw with the new disciples, that base could be experience in some prior job. This phase is applicable to both the newly graduated as well as someone moving into a new position or a new company with some degree of experience. Your prior training and experience will dictate how much guidance you will require and how much time you will spend in this phase of your career.

Earlier in the chapter we looked at some habits that you should work on especially in the Initiation Phase, as that is the time to begin to develop good habits. Because of their previous experience, the disciples showed such traits as taking responsibility, establishing good work habits, being reliable and dependable, performing with quality and praying daily. As they entered their new careers they certainly had to demonstrate service in a humble manner. As followers of John the Baptist, they had some idea of what to expect of the new organization they were joining. They had been listening intently as followers of John. They were obviously open to learning.

Yes, they had a lot of education ahead of them, but in many ways they had prepared themselves for their new roles with their own prior experience. They were now entering their new careers with some knowledge of what they were getting into. They each felt they were prepared to take on their new roles with the understanding that they had more to learn. They were excited about their new careers, just as you are about yours. While they knew they had a lot to learn, at this time they did not realize how much they had to learn. You are in this same position in your Initiation Phase.

When we follow the Gospels, we see that after Jesus has been baptized by John the Baptist, he spends time alone in the wilderness where he is tempted. He comes out of the wilderness and begins his ministry of teaching and healing. He gains many followers, and we see him specifically call the first four of those disciples who would become part of his inner circle. These four and others travel with Jesus as he preaches in Capernaum and throughout Galilee. Not only is he teaching, but he is also healing, as the numbers of his followers continues to grow. We witness him teaching to very large crowds, and those who would become his inner circle are listening and learning. A little later, we see the call of Matthew, the tax collector, to become a disciple. We then continue to see more teaching and healing as the group continues its travels. We witness their education in their new roles as disciples when we see Jesus teaching them a new way to look at religious law. They are sometimes taught clearly about such topics as murder, adultery, divorce, forgiveness, love, charity, prayer, worry and judgment among many other topics. It would seem that they are being taught the foundation of the new fulfillment of the law according to the teachings of Jesus.

While a lot of their time is spent learning, we do get to see some of their very early work in the Gospel of John. In John 4:1, we see that Jesus is gaining and baptizing more disciples than John the Baptist. It is further noted that *in fact it was not Jesus who baptized, but his disciples* (John 4:2 NIV). So while they are learning from Jesus, they are also working on his behalf handling entry level work following standards and procedures under the direction and approval of Jesus. Yes, they are initiates.

Heart of the Matter

1. The Initiation Phase
   - You are in an entry-level position as a new hire in you first job
   - This phase is a relatively short one in terms of your overall career
   - You may be feeling both confident and nervous at the same time in your early weeks
   - Now is the time to lay down a solid foundation of good habits
2. Habits to Practice
   - Honesty and integrity
   - Responsibility
   - Reliable and dependability
   - Quality
   - Patience
   - Humility
   - Prayer
3. Learn the company culture
4. Establish goals
5. You are in a continuous state of learning
6. Listen! This is a critical skill.
7. Organize yourself to be productive

4

Settling In
The Integration Phase

Do nothing from selfishness or empty conceit, but with humility of mind regard one another as more important than yourselves; do not merely look out for your own personal interests, but also for the interests of others (Philippians 2:3-4 NASB).

Exploring and Defining

Let's briefly review what the Integration Phase is all about. In this phase of your career you are doing more exploring and you are beginning to define yourself. You have developed a good understanding of your own roles and responsibilities in the work place. You are beginning to have a better personal understanding of yourself. You have been given greater latitude in your duties while still following standard operating procedures. Your work may have more depth and breadth than it did in the Initiation Phase.

You have developed a good working relationship with others on your team and have likely found your niche within the team. Some of your personal gifts and talents are beginning to show. You like to challenge yourself and seek out challenging assignments. While your confidence is increasing, there are still areas where additional training will be needed. Recognizing this will help you to remain grounded and not let some initial successes go to your head.

You might notice that there is some overlap with the Initiation Phase and the Integration Phase. Much of this depends upon your specific role and the expectations of your management. In some positions, typically a skilled or a specialty technical position, you may be required to complete a defined training or certification program. This may place you in in the Initiation Phase, but you are beginning to develop a better understanding of the business and yourself. So, yes, there will be some overlap in the first two phases.

You have likely had your first failure by now. It may have been some minor issue, but you probably felt really embarrassed about it. Or, it may have been a larger problem that was obvious to others on your team. This may have left you feeling a little unsure about yourself. Well, think about how you really felt. The most important point about failure is that you learn from it. Yes, it is embarrassing, or even worse. But, what did you learn from your failure? I don't care what it was, there is something to learn from it.

Has your mistake left you with a fear of failure and rejection? That is normal. What is not normal is to blow it off as no big deal. You may feel like you can ignore it and move on. You may think this makes you look strong, and you do want to look strong. But, you must face the failure head-on and learn from it. If you have the opportunity to discuss this with your manager, let him know what you learned from the situation. Let him know how you will handle a similar situation in the future. Show your strength by facing the failure, owning up to the problem and taking action to prevent it in the future. By doing this you are planning for success. This is extremely important. Facing your failure and learning from it allows you to deal with it in a mature manner and to move on from it without dwelling on it.

Let's take a look at some of the considerations of the Integration

Phase. You will see that you are continuing to build upon your experiences, however little they may be, of the Initiation Phase. However confident you may feel at this point, you still have a lot to learn through both additional experience and training. You cannot forget The Basics (Chapter 1) and you must continue to work on developing the good habits that we have already discussed.

Know Your Business

Getting to know the company was one of the topics discussed in the Initiation Phase. In the Integration Phase you are beginning to know the business. While these two things sound very similar, they are different. As you got to know the company, you began to know functions and responsibilities. You began to know where to go for specific needs with regard to your own responsibilities. But, a large part of getting to know the company in the Initiation Phase was getting to know the culture of the company.

In this Integration Phase you will begin to put all the pieces together and see into the belly of the beast. You will really know what your business is, how it is conducted and who your real customers are as you get beyond the marketing hype that defines your company and into the guts of how business is done.

As you learn the organizational structure, you will begin to understand the roles and responsibilities of others. In addition to learning the official structure, and thus who those in charge are, you will learn over time to know who the "informal" leaders are. There are always some "go-to" people outside of the organizational chart who can be valuable to you. You need to know who they are. That is not to say that you should bypass protocol, but you are learning how to work with others. Yes, you have a manager. You likely work as part of a group or team. There is always an informal leader in any group, however. Who is the person others go to with their quick questions? Who do they share their complaints with when they will not go to the boss? These are clues as to who the informal leader is.

Getting to know the business begins within your own work group. You operate within certain parameters as set by your position and the practices and procedures set forth for your position and your work group. As you begin to have some level of comfort in your position and with your co-workers, you start to see where some of the "rules" can be broken. You discover the short-cuts that can be taken in order to complete some process. These are safe short-cuts that have become the norm for some particular process. You may even have asked your supervisor about some of these and gotten the okay along with an explanation of why it is okay. Hopefully, you have been somewhat cautious and not stuck your neck out where it should not be. You begin to have some degree of latitude in accomplishing your tasks.

As you work closer with others you also begin to find out more about other work groups and other departments and divisions of your company. Perhaps you have assignments that take you into these other areas. As with your co-workers, you begin to see how the real work is accomplished. Pay attention to where the short-cuts are made and how they affect the product and the people.

If you should be in a position where you work directly with your company's customers, you will surely get a true picture of how your company is viewed from the outside. It may be different than what you thought from your initial research, your interview and your first impressions. Remember, they were selling the company image to you just as you were selling your image to them. Sometimes you will find that the image is what you had expected or even better. And, unfortunately, sometimes you will find it is not as good as you had thought.

Oftentimes, the sales department can tell you a lot about the business. How much "show" is put on for the customer to create an impression that has nothing to back it up? Are sales handled in an ethical manner? Is the customer really right? How are customers treated behind the scenes? How are the sales people compensated? Answers to these types of questions can be revealing about the business.

Also consider how your community views the business. Perhaps you relocated to a new city to begin your career. Now that you have been here for a while, talk to people you know in the community about their impressions of your company as a corporate citizen. Has your business come up in casual conversations, either good or bad? What do local newspapers or television news reports say about your company? Does your company have programs that support the community? As you become part of your community, you should have the opportunity to know and understand the answers to these types of questions.

When I went to work for Sprint, which was United Telephone at the time, the company was known to be a friendly family-like business. What I found unfolding was exactly that, and probably more so. I felt a lot of care at all levels including from the president who seemed to know every employee, including me. There was real care for employees at an individual level. I also found that the community in general saw the company as a very good corporate partner. The company did indeed give back in many ways to the community.

So, as I began to understand the business relationship with employees and with the community, I began to see the value that the business had for the same. It was a place that you felt good about working. In my case, my understanding of the business proved to be better than my expectations. For me, it was a good confirmation that I had made the right decision in coming to work for the company.

Unfortunately, you could find yourself on the other end of the spectrum. You could find that the company is far less than your expectations to the point of making you question your decision. Well, then you must make a decision. It will not be an easy one at this phase of your career. Weighing heavily may simply be the job market. You may have been fortunate to get the job in the first place. Finding a new job might not be so easy. Secondly, you do not have a lot of experience at this point in order to sell yourself to another company. If you have a family to also consider, then this can be even more difficult.

If you can go to work each day without knots in your stomach telling you that you should not be there, then, unless you do have some other great opportunity, stay the course. Continue to be the best employee that you can be. Listen and learn everything you can about your role and more. Maintain a good attitude, and maintain your confidence. Care for yourself well, physically and mentally. Continue to develop a stunning resume with your work ethic. Just because you work for a company that is less than what you thought does not mean that you should be any less than your very best.

As you work through this phase, you may even find that some of your early impressions of the business were wrong. It is possible that as you begin to know more, things could look better. Maybe higher level executives are aware of problems and are working on improvements. This, too, is part of knowing your business.

Know Yourself (Redux)

Knowing yourself is a lifelong process, and it did not end in the Initiation Phase. Hopefully by now you have had some projects to challenge your capabilities. How you handled these told you a lot about yourself. Maybe you even learned some things about yourself that you did not know by either successfully accomplishing them or in failing at the task. As you have probably heard so often, failure is a great teacher. Failure is one of the great opportunities to learn and improve. Take full advantage of every failure.

The other side of this is that maybe you have not been challenged. Maybe your assignments have been too easy. Well, now is the time to discuss this with your manager. You should have had some type of review process by now to assess how well you are doing. If you are feeling like you are not being challenged enough, then discuss this. There may be a reason why you are not being given greater challenges. Ask and find out what you could do to make this happen. Maybe you are simply in a standard new-hire process that everyone endures, or perhaps you have been doing something that is incorrect in some way. You won't know if you don't ask.

At this point you may be starting to feel like you should be having more responsibility. Part of this could be due to the fact that you are still new and green and ready to run at full speed. You may actually still need some training so that you run with a proper form and at a rate that will allow you to develop more fully. If you hear the words that you are simply not yet ready, you may feel this is a slight to your abilities. Try to gain an understanding of the company's expectations versus your own expectations. Once more, communications is a vital key to having a good understanding between you and your manager. Do not approach this issue in an indignant manner. Discussions about your career should be done in a calm manner with an understanding attitude. Later in your career, you will have the experience to know if you are having a problem with your manager, or if you are not being given a fair shake for some other reason. This early in your career, though, you are likely still being developed and groomed in the manner the company has planned for you.

Do you like yourself? Do you like who you are, how you act, how you treat others or how you take both praise and criticism? We all have something in us that we would like to change. Oftentimes we only look at the surface and see our outward features, our hair, our weight or our height. But, do you like who you are at the core? Do you like where your heart lies? *A good person produces good things from the treasury of a good heart* (Matthew 12:35 NLT). That is what you need to examine about yourself. At the core, while we may all be broken in some way, we are also created as good people. You probably have not gotten as far as you have by drifting away from some core of goodness. If you have, then the fact that you are reading this may mean that you are searching for your goodness.

There is nothing wrong with wanting to change our outward appearance for the better. There is also nothing wrong with wanting to change our hearts. Tap into that goodness that you have inside. Let it shine. Be true to who you really are at your foundation of goodness.

As you integrate yourself into your work group and into the business, you may find yourself trying to fit in by acting like those around you. If they have good hearts, that is good; if their hearts are not in the right place, then it is not the way for you. Again, you may not like these people, but you do have to work with them. Maybe your goodness will influence them. You must remain true to yourself.

Finally, let's talk again about goals. This topic was brought up in the Initiation Phase as an important consideration. As your career develops, setting your career goals becomes ever increasingly important. You should be sitting down with your manager to establish goals for the coming year. You should also be reviewing your goals with your manager on a regular basis, not just at the end of the year. If this is not being done, then ask to meet with your manager to informally discuss your goals at least once per quarter. You should not be surprised at the end of the year with your manager's rating of your performance.

Hopefully, you are being more involved in setting your goals with your manager. Up to now, you may have had them established for you. However, some managers may further delay getting your take on the goals until you are in the Transition Phase. It is not a problem to approach your manager about your ability to have more input to your goals. Let your manager know, for example, if there are areas where you would like additional training. Be prepared to explain why, and be ready to put in the work to achieve your goals.

Maybe you are not getting the opportunity to have much input to your goals at this point. Maybe your company does not include personal goals and long-term goals in your annual goal-setting process. (By the way, most companies will have some name for this process, usually some sort of acronym that defines the process.) You can, and should, be writing down your personal goals annually. This includes looking out from one to five years as well. You want to be looking at your future as you understand it at this time. Review your previous goals and adjust as necessary depending upon your growth, experiences and needs. Again, there is plenty written on this whole process. Do your homework!

Become a People Person

In the Initiation Phase, I talked about the need for good listening skills. Part of developing good listening skills is simply giving the speaker your full attention. I also stressed the importance of remembering people's names. Continuing to work on these skills is no less important now. While you are developing your communications skills, you are also developing your relationship skills. As you grow along your career path, your interaction with others and how you handle yourself is going to be a key to your success.

In one of his leadership books, *Be a People Person*, author John C. Maxwell covers this topic very well. Since this is a key trait of being a good leader, it is something you must develop and practice ... beginning now. Being a people person is not something that you can fake. There are people who simply have the personality that makes them a good people person. You know the type. You enjoy being around them. People gravitate to them. If they are not the official leader in a group, they may be an unofficial leader. They simply relate well to others. Maxwell sums it up nicely, however, with these words:

"What's the key to relating to others? It's putting yourself in someone else's place instead of putting them in their place. Christ gave the perfect rule for establishing quality human relationships. We call it the Golden Rule, a name it got sometime around the seventeenth century. Near the end of the Sermon on the Mount, Christ summed up a series of profound thoughts on human conduct by saying, *Therefore treat people the same way you want them to treat you* (Matthew 7:12 NASB).

"In this brief command, Christ taught us a couple of things about developing relationships with others. We need to decide how we want to be treated. Then we need to begin treating others in that manner" (Maxwell 2007, pp. 13-14).

What we call the Golden Rule is possibly the best-known quote from the Bible and is the standard Jesus set for dealing with other people. If we wish to be loved, we must give love. If we wish to be respected, we must respect all persons, even those we dislike. If we wish to be forgiven, we must also forgive. If we wish others to speak kindly of us, we must speak kindly of them and avoid gossip.

You have met and worked with your co-workers and perhaps with others outside of your work group by now. In business today, you are likely to be engaged in collaborative efforts. You need to be able to work with others and respect opinions even when they differ from your own. You also need to be able to support your own views and share them clearly and confidently. Being a people person is not about giving in, nor is it about forcing your views on others. It is about developing relationships. If you are having trouble with this, then by all means pursue some training in interpersonal relationships. If your department or your company does not want to provide this training, then pursue it on your own. Again, there are plenty of books and websites devoted to this subject. More homework for you!

Can you work for someone you do not like or respect? It may not be a lot of fun, but look at the challenge as an opportunity. I recall working for a manager whose personal and moral views where completely opposite of my own. Unfortunately, being the good people person that I was, he enjoyed sharing with me. I heard more about his personal life than I ever wanted to know. There were times when I told him this, but he really needed someone to talk to. And maybe in some small way he was looking for someone to tell him that what he was doing was wrong. I was not mature enough at that time to explicitly tell him he was wrong, but I tried to let him see this by my actions.

Regardless of my views of him personally, I did my utmost best in the work I performed. This in no way meant that I was supporting his views, but rather I was supporting the work that needed to be done. Sometimes you need to separate the two. I had others ask me how I could work for him. I could only explain that I had a job to do, and he was not going to hold me back. I got great reviews from him. I got great references from him when I moved on to another position. And, I will share later how he supported me when I was losing my job.

The same applies to working with co-workers. You are not going to like everyone you work with. (Oh, and not everyone is going to like you!) Look at this as a great opportunity to improve upon your inter-personal skills. Maybe it is a good time to test some of the skills you are trying to learn or improve upon. If you can work well with someone in this situation, then how much better will you work with those with whom you have a good relationship. Just remember that you are not likely to change this individual. Just be firm in your own beliefs and don't be led astray.

Here are some final thoughts on being a people person with a few simple behaviors you can work on. This is not by any means any exhaustive list, but these are simple, easy actions you can take.

- **Be positive**. Look for the good in every situation. Don't be dragged down by the negativity of others. When possible, sur-round yourself with other positive people. Look for solutions to problems.

- **Practice good manners**. Remember "please" and "thank-you." You are never above being polite. Even in heated exchanges, you can be the bigger person and remain cool and calm.

- **Be engaging**. Think about what draws you to listen to some-one else. You likely have some similar traits. Maybe you just need to work on them and bring them out. Be easy to talk to. Oh, and listen!

- **Ask questions**. This is necessary to clarify assignments, under-stand instructions and develop a better working knowledge of your organization. It is also an opportunity to display your interest in a situation, a problem or a person. Ask others about their interests.

- **Take breaks with others**. Simply spending a few minutes of down time with others can be rewarding as you get to know them. This is a good opportunity to practice some of the other things in this list. It is a time to share your interests with others so they can see who you are. I will admit, early in my career I was not good at this. I felt like I would be showing a strong work ethic by not taking a break. I further justified this by the fact that I was a shy individual. It would take me a while to learn the value of this.

- **Volunteer.** You may be doing volunteer work in your personal life. Your business may also provide opportunities to volunteer your services through company-sponsored charity events. Whether you volunteer in your personal life or in your business life, it is a good way to develop quality interpersonal skills.

- **Assess yourself.** Look at yourself as others might. Would you enjoy being around someone like you? Would you enjoy working with someone like you? Do you find yourself being argumentative? What don't you like about yourself? Look into ways to improve areas where you may be lacking. At the same time, look at how can you build upon those parts of your personality that are your strengths.

Not Everyone Likes You

To state the obvious, we all have unique personalities. We also all have a unique set of gifts and talents. You, first of all, need to accept the differences in others. It is easy to see the flaws in others, but you must work on your own flaws first. And, instead of looking for the flaws in others, look for the good in them. See what you can learn from them.

So, be aware that not everyone is going to be completely accepting of who you are. Be self-aware. Look hard at yourself to see if what someone else does not accept about you is a problem. Check yourself to see if you may be displaying some persona that might be offensive to others. If so, then set out a plan to correct it. You are still developing good work ethics and habits, so adjustment as needed is a good thing. However, you may also find that others are jealous of you in some way.

Perhaps you have displayed some gifts or talents or strengths that they do not have. They may be jealous of your abilities, or worse, they may be threatened. It may not even be over your talents. It could be your looks, your position, your salary, your success, or any number of things. Jealousy and feeling that you are a threat are not that uncommon, especially in a competitive position.

When I began my career, I did not know that I was the first individual in the work group who was a degreed college graduate. Now, while I did not make a big deal of my degree, the others in the work group were being highly critical of me because of this. I did not know this at the time. It was only after I began to know the team better and know myself better that I became aware of this. I then did my utmost to ensure I did not bring up my degree in any way; although, I had not done so prior to this time. But now being aware of the situation, I went out of my way to avoid the entire issue. Instead, I worked at being a good people person and a good servant to the others at every opportunity. It is important to note that this should not be confused with trying to "buy" my way into the group or change who I was. I remained true to the core of myself after evaluating the situation. I looked at it as more of an opportunity to express who I was as a good and caring person.

Now, you do not want to handle this as I did when I was in grade school. (See, even what you learned way back then can apply later in life.) I was a top student at school. Not only was I getting top grades, but I was also getting various awards for my school activities. Then I discovered that there was a group of kids who looked down on me for getting good grades and making them look bad. Unfortunately, this bothered me to the point that I had to make a change. I did not remain true to who I was. Instead, I started hanging out with some of the "bad" kids. I joined in their activities and got myself in a lot of trouble numerous times. I thought that if I acted like them, they would like me and all would be well in the world. It didn't quite work out that way. You must remain true to yourself, maintain your honesty, integrity and ethics, and look for opportunities to serve others and improve yourself.

Entrepreneurial Spirit

I want to say a few words about entrepreneurship. We usually wrap this word around someone who starts a new business venture. Of course, we only think of it with regard to those entrepreneurs who were successful! Many have failed. Many successful entrepreneurs failed many times before succeeding. We typically associate entrepreneurship with someone who is willing to take risks. In the Integration Phase, you are exploring and trying to define yourself. We have discussed planning, organizing, communicating and other skills important to your career. If you have an entrepreneurial spirit, you may feel that some of these things don't apply to you. You want to spread your wings, beat your own drum, play your own tune. If this is you, hopefully it was important enough that you selected a company and a position that would allow you to develop in an entrepreneurial environment.

I will tell you, however, that an entrepreneur must be well-organized, have extremely good planning skills and must be a top-notch communicator. Yes, everything we have been discussing so far applies to you. When you are pursuing your own way as an entrepreneur you had better be well-organized to a fault and communicate to the degree of the best salesperson you can think of. Many people do not develop that entrepreneurial spirit until they have had experience in a business environment. They use their experience and their developed skills to pursue their new career path. The skills we have discussed require a lot of discipline. Entrepreneurs are very disciplined in their pursuit of their vision. There are many other characteristics that entrepreneurs have in common, but the point I want to make is that those skills you need to develop for a successful career will serve you well no matter the path you take.

While the term entrepreneur is typically used regarding a new business venture, it can also be used to describe teams within an organization. Even simple group meetings can be entrepreneurial in spirit when leaders are seeking new ideas with brainstorming. You can even be entrepreneurial to some degree as an individual when you accept a new challenge that allows you some latitude in how to proceed. In these cases you put yourself out there a little bit, take some ownership and have "some skin in the game" as you accept some degree of risk.

I had several great entrepreneurial experiences in my career at Sprint. One of the earlier ones was when I was managing our business product mix at United Telephone of Indiana. The executive team wanted new fresh ideas on profitable, non-regulated products and services. (The telecommunications industry was highly regulated, and this was a time when deregulation was taking place allowing the industry to pursue new opportunities.) The executive team encouraged the formation of small entrepreneurial teams from anywhere in the company to develop ideas. The company allowed the teams to meet as often as they wanted as long as our regular daily work did not suffer. It sounds like it was merely extra work, but this had really fired up the workforce.

With a data background, I was part of a group focused on data products and services. As we brainstormed, we eventually had a few ideas rise to the top. We had to organize and develop these ideas to the greatest detail. We had to prepare a complete business plan covering every aspect of a new product/service from development and launch through the complete product life-cycle. We then had to present these business plans before the executive team as well as the other entrepreneurial teams. Ultimately many plans were approved and developed, including that of my team. I believe it was this very experience that set me on a path that would ultimately lead me to my own business several years later.

I felt quite fortunate to have been placed in a position that allowed the entrepreneurial process to take place. It was challenging and rewarding. It involved commitment and risk-taking. It forced me to sharpen every facet of my business skills. I would later recall this experience when seeking solutions within my own teams, giving them ownership with responsibility, challenge with reward, and skill development with a future vision.

Balance

As in your Initiation Phase, you may still be trying to make that good first impression. You may be the first one at work in the morning and the last one to leave in the evening. In a salaried position, you may be putting in a lot of extra hours. If you are not in a salaried position but are rather in an hourly position, then this may not be an issue. In an hourly position, you would not be working overtime without prior authorization. However, some will work and not charge the company for it. How much time at work is enough? How much is too much? Are you putting in the extra hours because of the need, or are you doing it to try to impress others and make yourself look good?

Now, some companies will expect this of you, and other companies will discourage it. So, be aware of your company culture. You should certainly understand this by now, and maybe you have made an adjustment in this area already. If your company expects this of you, then how much is expected? At some point you have to make a decision about the balance in your life. Remember **Rule 4**: you need to take some time off to recharge your batteries. Then there is **Rule 5**: honor your mother and father, and all of those who care about you — your spouse and your family. Finally, you must consider **Rule 10**: are you working to get more because you see what others have and you want it too? You must learn to live within your means.

You must also realize that more work does not necessarily equate to quality work. Quality work completed on time is what employers are looking for. So, putting hours in just to look good to your manager is a very bad choice. If you are putting in the hours in order to complete a project on time and with quality, then maybe it is required. Realize, however, that it should not be required for every project you work on. If you find this to be the case, then speak with your manager. Maybe there are areas where you need help, direction or additional training.

Balance between personal life and business life is very important. Having Christ as the one foundation to build upon for both your personal life and your career will avoid pitfalls and traps. You will not split yourself into two different people depending on where you are and what you are doing. Family is more important than money. Sure, you have bills to pay and a family to feed. Have you put together a budget? More importantly, is that budget based upon your income? That is to say, you should not be spending beyond your means and incurring great debt. Once again, there are plenty of good books and websites on this topic. One popular author and radio show host who comes to mind when discussing debts and budgets is Dave Ramsey. If you are a follower of Christ, then you have likely heard of him.

Remember, *No one can serve two masters. Either you will hate the one and love the other, or you will be devoted to the one and despise the other* (Matthew 6:24 NIV). Don't destroy yourself by trying to live beyond your means. It is not healthy. You will find your mind and your efforts being torn to chase the dollar. You will sacrifice your wife, your children, your health, and your ability to serve others with your gifts and talents. Others may actually see the intrinsic value in you as you display your ability to live within your means. This demonstrates your ability to understand your situation, to practice restraint and self-control, to organize, to work within set requirements, and to have a vision to the future. It says a lot of good things about you.

I worked with a salesperson who lived well outside of his means. He drove very nice cars and wore expensive suits. He always appeared on top of his game. He actually was a good salesperson. He did not need to put on a front of success. He was successful in his own right. However, he was also in great debt. He asked to borrow money from me on more than one occasion. He would go out of his way to pick up a dinner bill, even when I knew he was maxing out his credit card.

Sure, he made pretty good money. He was also divorced. His small house was mortgaged to the hilt. Debt collectors were calling him. He would promise payments that he couldn't make. His personal life was a shambles. None of this had to be. He kept chasing the dollar to tremendous personal loss. I had a few casual conversations with him about getting his finances under control. I am not sure any of it ever took.

The Twelve Disciples

We saw how the disciples traveled with Jesus and witnessed as he taught and healed many. It is in the Integration Phase that we see Jesus select the twelve disciples who will be his close companions and form the inner circle of disciples. The Gospel of Luke tells us that he went off by himself to pray and spent the night alone before returning to select the twelve. He calls them together in the Gospel of Matthew and gives them the authority to drive out impure spirits and heal the sick. When they were in the Initiation Phase, the disciples traveled with Jesus and saw him proclaiming the kingdom of God and healing the sick and diseased. Now we begin to see the first hint of an expansion of their roles in their new careers as they are given additional responsibility.

Matthew continues to tell us that Jesus sent out the twelve disciples with some very specific instructions. They are specifically to go to the "lost sheep of Israel" to proclaim Jesus' message. In fact, they are specifically instructed not to go to the areas of Gentiles at this time. They are then told that they can heal the sick, raise the dead and drive out demons. Many other details are provided on how they are to proceed on their first mission. In fact, they are prepared for the reality that not everyone will be receptive to their teaching (not everyone will like them!). Finally, we see in the Gospel of Luke that when they return from their first mission, they report to Jesus all that they had done.

So, we see them integrating into their new roles with expanded responsibilities. They have been formed into a team with a clear understanding of their role. They obviously must have a somewhat clear working relationship with one another by this time. They are beginning to have some idea of where they fit in within Jesus' ministry. And, of course, Jesus is checking on their progress all the time.

We also see in the Gospel of Luke that after the twelve returned from their mission, Jesus sent out seventy-two disciples on another mission. Their mission was to go ahead of Jesus to prepare for his travel to those towns. Again, very specific instruction were provided to this group. They returned and reported to Jesus with the joy of their experience. Some histories suggest that Matthias, who would later replace Judas Iscariot as one of the twelve, was among this group of seventy-two (McBirnie 2004, p. 184).

So, perhaps many of the disciples were being tested. Maybe they were on that fast-track program that is sometimes used to weed out the field and find the best candidates. We later see in the Gospel of John that some of the disciples found some parts of his teaching difficult to follow. It says that they "grumbled." John 6:66 (NIV) tells us that *From this time many of his disciples turned back and no longer followed him.* Jesus asks the twelve if they too want to leave. Simon Peter answers for the group when he professes his belief in Jesus as the Messiah.

After their first mission on their own, the disciples continued to be taught by Jesus as they traveled. Jesus now teaches them more frequently through parables, forty of which are recorded in the gospels. The parables cover many facets of life, and the disciples see their old ways of thinking turned upside down. Jesus often has to explain the parables to the twelve disciples as they continue in their learning process. They were also witnesses to an increasing number of miracles including feeding of 5,000 followers, Jesus (and Simon Peter) walking on water, driving out demons, healings and ultimately resurrection of the dead. The disciples eventually see that the Jewish leaders are troubled by Jesus' actions as well as his claims.

His closest followers also listen as Jesus predicts his own suffering and death. At this point they still do not understand this part of his mission, and Simon Peter vows that he would never let this happen. It is also around this time that Jesus asks the disciples who they think that he is. Still not quite getting it, some of the disciples argue about which one of them is the greatest. Of course, Jesus uses this as a teaching moment.

The twelve disciples see that the chief priests and elders question Jesus' authority. They are fully vested in Jesus' teachings and are concerned for his safety. They all remain with him ... except one who agrees to betray him and deliver him over to the chief priests.

The twelve who Jesus selected to be his core had managed to learn and to deal with difficulties and to work as a team. They understood they still had much to learn; they asked questions. They saw that their new roles were bigger than themselves and that they would need to put the needs of others before their own. While they had given up much for a greater good, they were settling in with their new roles, perhaps with a greater conviction.

Heart of the Matter

1. The Integration Phase
   - You are continuing to explore the business and define yourself
   - You have a good understanding of your roles and responsibilities
   - You have developed a good working relationship with your team
   - Your personal gifts and talents are beginning to show
   - While your confidence is increasing, you continue to be in a learning process
   - You have likely experienced your first failure
2. Develop an awareness of the "informal" structure within your business
3. Understand the relationship that the business has with its employees and with the community
4. Personal relationship skills must be learned and practiced
5. Remember the Golden Rule
6. The entrepreneurial spirit — organize, plan, communicate
7. Remember **Rules 4, 5 and 10**
8. Do not live beyond your means

5

Finding Your Voice
The Transition Phase

Consider it pure joy, my brothers and sisters, whenever you face trials of many kinds, because you know that the testing of your faith produces perseverance. Let perseverance finish its work so that you may be mature and complete, not lacking anything (James 1:2-4 NIV).

Is the Thrill Gone?

You have spent your time being engaged in your work, establishing relationships with co-workers, and learning more about your company. As you have handled increasing responsibilities you have gained confidence in your abilities. You have grown, you have matured, you have gained new knowledge and you have learned how to deal with new experiences. You have integrated yourself into the business. Your thoughts may now be running to advancement. You have been given those opportunities to prove yourself to your management. You may have gained experience as a project or team leader. You may actually be in a supervisory position at this time.

You seem to be excelling in your niche. You may be learning to take some calculated risks, but you still need to use some caution. By now, your input has been sought in establishing team goals or in addressing some specific issue. As you are more involved in setting your goals, you need to ensure you are re-establishing your 1-5 year goals, which may have changed several times at this phase.

At this time, good or bad, you may have been placed on a career track by your employer. You might be considered a career professional where you are performing a variety of duties and working on problems of a moderate scope where analysis of situations or data requires a review of a variety of factors. You are using professional concepts and applying company policies and procedures to resolve routine issues. You have some degree of autonomy in your decision making.

Or, you may be in a skilled position where you are performing a variety of duties that involve related steps, methods or application of standard practices and specific instructions with occasional variations. You are performing basic research and analysis of information without a lot of supervision.

You may be in a specialty or technical position using advanced and specialized knowledge to perform unique and/or complex technical tasks or activities.

Finally, you may be in a supervisory role providing immediate supervision of a group of employees. You might be assigning tasks, reviewing work at frequent intervals and maintaining schedules. Your planning and organizing skills are beginning to broaden.

Hopefully, wherever you find yourself at this point, you feel your abilities are being put to good use. As the first days, weeks, months and years of your new career rolled on, you settled in and perhaps have found a routine that works for you. You may feel very comfortable in your role. This may last for some time. But, what happens when that thrill wears off? Things seem mundane. You don't feel like your talents are being properly used. Maybe you have had a small promotion or two, but you feel ready to move up to something bigger. You are anxious to make some larger upward steps. You don't feel you've been given the opportunity to shine. You may feel jealous of others. Maybe you are beginning to feel like you are being held back, especially as you see others advancing around you.

You may even wonder if you made the wrong decision in coming to work for this particular company. Do they really value you? Or, maybe you have seen a side of the company that you did not see earlier, and you are not happy. Maybe the company has undergone a transition with new management or consolidations or mergers. There are a lot of ways that your company could have changed and not be the same company that you went to work for.

Change Versus Transition

You are in a transition mode. The thing about a transition is that it is different than change. You may have experienced changes in your career and in your personal life. As just stated, you may have had the opportunity to lead a project or a team. You may be in a supervisory or lower level management role. Those have been changes. All of these changes have come together to place you in a position of transition.

Transition is defined as "a movement, development, or evolution from one form, stage, or style to another" (*Merriam-Webster*). Some synonyms include evolution, growth, passage and transformation (Thesaurus.com). I like the way author William Bridges talks about transition in his book *Managing Transitions*. He says that change is situational, a function that takes place to its completion. He says that transition, on the other hand, is psychological, a process that people go through. In this process they deal with emotion. Now, Bridges is discussing transition with regard to transitions in the business itself. In a business transition he talks about three phases of transition. In the early phase, there is a letting go of the old ways. There is an acknowledgment of the impending change. In the final phase there is a commitment to functioning in the new environment. It is the middle phase that might best describe our career Transition Phase. In this phase there is some uncertainty and anxiety. At the same time, however, you can see new possibilities and embrace new visions (Bridges 2009).

Let's take a look at how this might play-out for you. You are in the process of finding your own voice and becoming more independent in your thinking. Your ideas seem to have more merit since you have paid your dues in the Initiation and Integration Phases. Your value to the company is increasing and has manifested itself in merit increases and promotions. You recognize that you have gotten beyond the first two career phases. You can see the possibilities for your future, but there is that bit of uncertainty. Have you really had enough differing experiences? Have your changes expanded and broadened your understanding of the business enough? Are there still some areas in which you are not really comfortable? Do you still feel underutilized? Have you had a failure or two that make you question your readiness? Is there someone whose style you admire, but you do not feel you measure up? Does your career seem to be moving at a snail's pace compared to your expectations?

Any of these scenarios implies a transition that is not comfortable for you. It is not necessarily a result of anything you have done. It could be that you are growing as you gain experience, it could be that you have been placed in a more challenging position that you find uncomfortable, it could be that you are not challenged enough, it could be that you are no longer getting the personal attention that you did in the earlier phases of your career, or it could be that the company has changed. There are a lot of reasons that you may not be comfortable where you are at this time. In a marriage, this has been called the "seven year itch," a term that suggests that happiness in a relationship declines after around year seven of a marriage. It represents a rough patch in a marriage. You may just feel you are in a rough patch in your career.

You may also be facing changes and even transitions in your personal life that affect your view of your career. Maybe you were previously single and have married. Maybe you have started a family. Perhaps you were married and have gone through a divorce. Possibly you have lost a loved one. You have experienced changes in circumstances, attitudes and relationships. There are many changes and transitions in our lives, and wherever they originate, they can affect all areas of our lives by adding stress.

There are, however, also reasons that you may be quite happy at this time. Perhaps you have received a nice promotion or two and are doing something you just love. Maybe the company is everything you expected and more. The pay is great, the hours are great, the team is great. How fortunate you are! You may be feeling so good that you do not have a great awareness of your transition. It may all feel simply natural to you. If you have a good, healthy outlook, then you see the obstacles you have run into as being there to strengthen and season you. You fall into that group of people who see the Transition Phase with a vision full of possibilities.

But I believe that for more of us than not, we will at some point feel that something is just a little off. It may be the big things just discussed, or it might just be a small gnawing of minor activities, events, relationships or changes at home. Maybe things have been so good that a new boss or a new team seems somewhat lacking. You could even be concerned that things are so good that you do not want them to change. But in the back of your mind, you know that change is inevitable. Regardless of your circumstances, I do not think it is uncommon to feel some degree of unease.

You have found out who you are, what drives you and what gives you that feeling of accomplishment. You have become more confident in your decisions and choices. Some of your new-found insight will lead you to question your current circumstances. Perhaps you had set some long-term goals that you feel you should be reaching, but you have not achieved them. And, of course, the other side may be that you have achieved your long-term goals already and feel ready to move forward.

It is sort of like the opening paragraph of Charles Dickens' *A Tale of Two Cities*, "It was the best of times, it was the worst of times, it was the age of wisdom, it was the age of foolishness ..." Perhaps things have gone so well for you that you have gained a confidence that you feel empowers you to do more, to pursue greater things, to move on elsewhere if needed. As a result of things going so well, you feel that the only way to go farther is to leave the company because there is no further opportunity here. Perhaps in your wisdom, you will make a foolish move. So, now is not the time to make a rash decision. It is a time for reflection and prayer for guidance.

I am not saying that it is not time to move on; I am only saying that your feelings that things are not quite right for you are not untypical for this time in your career. You need to take some time and evaluate yourself and your situation. What might you consider? Are you doing work that you truly enjoy? Are you only wanting more because you have seen others move up? Are you truly ready for your next upward move? Should you consider a lateral move within the company to broaden your scope and knowledge of the business (rather than leaving the business)? Are your goals realistic? Take a good look at them and update them if necessary. Are you bored with your work? Are you overworked? What are the reasons for feeling this way? Are you not receiving the training you feel you need? Has the company direction changed such that you are uncomfortable with it? What are your options if you do want to make a change? How will this affect not only you but also your family? Have you discussed these things with your manager? If you cannot discuss them with your manager, then that indicates a problem. You need to consider these types of questions. If you cannot answer them, then you need to ponder them in a deeper fashion. That is, you need to pray about it. *If you want to know what God wants you to do, ask him, and he will gladly tell you, for he is always ready to give a bountiful supply of wisdom to all who ask him; he will not resent it* (James 1:5 TLB).

Answer all of your questions. Gather all of the facts. Think long and hard. Pray. Remember **Rules 1** and **10**. If there is not an immediate need to make a decision, then take your time. There is no reason not to think this through thoroughly. If you do make a decision to leave the company, then develop a plan for yourself to do this. And most importantly, continue to do your best and maintain your integrity at your current position. First of all, it is the right thing to do. Your employer has invested in you, and there is no reason not to give them your best. And, secondly, you absolutely do not want to burn any bridges behind you. You may find yourself trying to come back to this company one day. This happened to me twice, so I know of what I speak.

I left United Telephone Company of Indiana and went to work for one of our sister companies in Florida. I left because I felt like I was at a bit of a dead end. My goals were high, and I was not moving up as fast as I felt I should. I saw two levels of management above me, and neither individual had any plans to move up, across or out. I was in the Transition Phase of my career for sure. So, I made the decision to take a small advancement to a position at our sister company in Florida. The VP of Operations told me before I left that if I ever wanted to come back, just give him a call. Well, my move to Florida was done, perhaps, a little rashly. After about two-and-a-half years, I made the call. I was generously able to return to the Indiana company at my then-current position. It was made possible because of the quality of my work, my work ethic and my integrity. I did not compromise any of those when I left the Indiana company, or while I was with the Florida company.

I have researched and read numerous articles on actions that will negatively impact your career, including a LinkedIn post from former GE chairman and CEO Jack Welch entitled *10 Behaviors that Could Kill Your Career*. (I don't know why these things are always posed in the negative sense.) Every list has its own twist on the career-killing activities. Some actions are very obvious, and some are worded to be obtuse. You could easily take these lists of 8, 10, 12 or 15 items and have a list of 100. When I studied these lists, however, I saw some common threads running through all of them. It is a simple matter of getting back to the basics. And, importantly, *you* are in charge of *your* career. It is not your supervisor or your manager or your company who is managing your career; it is you.

So, here is my list of **Seven Ways to Boost Your Career**. (I like to be positive.) And, as you will see, I have already touched on most, if not all of them, in some way. It is good to be reminded of these in the Transition Phase of your career.

1. Maintain your honesty, integrity, ethics and trustworthiness
2. Practice open communications — remember listening takes precedence
3. Be a team player; respect the opinions of others
4. Be a humble servant
5. Always be learning and be open to change
6. Maintain your personal care and growth
7. Establish clear goals

Developing a Servant's Heart

No matter what your job is or what position you hold, you are providing a service. Whether you are an accountant or an engineer, a supervisor or a CEO, a sales rep or a project manager, you are providing a service. I have not been able to think of one job that is not a service job. Sure, you may be in manufacturing, education, healthcare, finance or any other industry, but whatever particular role you are in, you are providing a service to someone. You, specifically you, have customers. They may not be external customers, but you always have internal customers. Whatever you are doing you are providing something for someone. It could be accounting reports for executives, it could be technical support for end users in your company, it could be engineering designs for those who manufacture your products, it could be supporting your team as a leader, but you do provide a product or service for your particular customers.

One simple definition of service is the action of helping or doing work for someone. So, whether for someone internal to or external to your company, you are providing a service. And as one who provides a service, what does that make you? A servant, of course! Again, a simple definition says that a servant is a person who performs duties for others. You see, like it or not, we are all servants. As an employee you are simply a servant (a person who works for another person) who gets paid a wage or a salary. Now, how we perform in our role as servants, or employees, is a key issue in our development both as individuals and as employees.

So, let's take a look at this thing called servanthood. Consider Jesus himself: *For even the Son of Man did not come to be served, but to serve* (Mark 10:45 NIV). One of the central themes of the Bible is the servanthood of Jesus. Here he was going about and gathering a ragtag band together. He was the most charismatic leader imaginable; yet, in everything he emphasized his role as a servant. *Who, being in very nature God, did not consider equality with God something to be used to his own advantage; rather, he made himself nothing by taking the very nature of a servant, being made in human likeness* (Philippians 2:6-7 NIV). Further, he tells us very specifically that to really excel, our actions should be those of a servant. He even says that when you are in a position to be in charge of others, you have a particular responsibility to conduct yourself as such: *But Jesus called the disciples and said, "You know that the rulers of the unbelievers lord it over them and their superiors act like tyrants over them. That's not the way it should be among you. Instead, whoever wants to be great among you must be your servant"* (Matthew 20:25-26 ISV).

I will not say that this concept was in my mind as I started my own career. But, I was raised in a manner to treat others fairly, to apply the Golden Rule. I was also a good listener. People would often come to me with their personal problems because they needed someone to talk to, to confide in, without fear of judgment, or even worse, that their troubled tale would leak out. Over time, I found that as I developed as a better manager, I was becoming a servant to those who worked for me. Whatever the particular level of management or area of management, a large part of my job was to make it easier for those who reported to me to do their job with the fewest number of roadblocks. I had to manage upward to change policies and procedures, streamlining them and eliminating redundancy and outdated requirements. I listened to the needs of others and went to bat to make it easier for them to do their jobs successfully. I did not do this at the expense of others. As I grew in breadth, I had enough knowledge to know how changes could affect those outside my sphere of influence. In fact, I often improved things for areas outside of my own responsibility as well.

It was sometime in the early 2000s when a book came out about servant-leadership. I think it may have been Ken Blanchard's book *The Servant Leader*. It was highly touted as the new way to lead in the corporate world. It was encouraged reading within the company. When I checked it out, I found out that this was how I was already managing. It was my management style; it now had a name!

There are now numerous good books about servant-leaders. I am not going to recommend a particular book. Do the work. Look into some of them. I think you will get the idea. True leadership is accomplished through servanthood.

It is in the Transition Phase of your career where you will begin to see leadership development. You may have your first experience as a project leader, or maybe you have taken a supervisory position, or you may already be in a lower level management position. Especially if you were in a fast-track management program, you have likely had some type of leadership training by now. Or, you may have been placed in a position as a project leader or team leader to see how you handle a leadership role. If you get a big head and lord it over others, you will be a failure as a leader. If you lead by example (honesty, integrity, ethics, good communications skills) you will have a better chance for success.

Now, do not confuse servant-leadership with doing everything for your team or not holding them responsible to meet the team objectives. Just the opposite. You include them in the discussion of the expectations. You ensure they understand the scope of the project. You ask about roadblocks and try to knock them down for the team. You do your best to ensure they have all the right tools for the job. You encourage them, and you hold them accountable just as you hold yourself accountable. And, you listen ... a lot.

Leader Versus Manager

As I stated earlier, you may be in some form of a supervisory or management position by this time in your career if that is the path you are pursuing. Having a title with either of those words does not necessarily make you a leader. A supervisor is an individual who is in charge of something or someone (*Merriam-Webster*). A manager handles or directs with some degree of skill (*Merriam-Webster*).

In such a position, you may be handing out work assignments and monitoring their completion in a timely manner. You may have to prepare reports for your own manager. At this level you are following standard procedures in supervising or managing the group assigned to you. If you are in one of those skilled positions, then you may have been placed in the role because of your outstanding technical capabilities. It is hoped that you will provide guidance for those within your group to help them advance their skills.

You provide some degree of control and order for your group. You find that your organization and planning skills are now being put to the test as you are responsible for team results. This is a good thing as it will help you to refine these skills. It is a part of your transition into the Leadership Phase.

As you work with your team, you will also have the opportunity to practice and hone your communication skills. You will need to be sure that your directions and assignments to your team are clear and concise. You will also find that you are practicing your interpersonal relationship skills as you have to deal with others in a different manner. You may not be their friend, but you must be the person they can talk to freely and share their thoughts and opinions without fear of some repercussion. You will be developing your listening skills.

So many of the basics that have been discussed up to now are becoming more important and gaining breadth. You will need to start thinking from a broader perspective as you see activities and projects and people from a little different angle. You have been provided with an opportunity to work on the basics, and you need to take every advantage of this opportunity. Remember that you are growing. You are transitioning into the Leadership Phase. It will be easy to try to over-supervise and over-manage your team. This is not uncommon for your first opportunity in this type of role. You might feel the need to come on strong to show your strength. In your first or second supervisory position, you are still learning. You are working at becoming a leader. Now is not the time to be brash or brazen or reckless. Monitor yourself closely. Check yourself. Question yourself. Recall the Golden Rule. Listen.

We will discuss more about leadership in the next chapter.

It's OK to Fire Someone

I was torn between addressing this issue in this chapter or in the Leadership Phase chapter. After some thought, I came to the realization that you may still be in the Transition Phase when you need to take this action. Yes, you will likely have to fire someone at some point in your career. That is, of course, if you are in a supervisory, management or executive level position. If you are an "unofficial" leader such as a SME (subject matter expert) or a team leader without the responsibility of hiring and firing, then you will not be in this position. But if you are in a position to hire and fire, then it is as okay to fire someone as it is to hire someone. Firing someone is a little more difficult than hiring someone, however.

There are a couple of general situations in which you may be involved in the letting go of an employee. The first is that of an employee who has performed poorly over time, or who has performed some single action that is grounds for immediate dismissal. Your company should have an employee handbook in some form that identifies the process involved for each type of situation. For a poorly performing employee, there are likely procedures to be followed to document the poor performance as well as a performance improvement plan. Causes for immediate dismissal of an employee should also be very clearly laid out by your company. Regardless of the situation, there are federal and state laws which also must be followed. Your human resources team should make these very clear as well.

The other situation that you may encounter is a general downsizing of the business. In this case, there is no specific reason to fire a particular employee other than the fact that you need to cut some number of employees from your team. As with the situation of a poor performing employee, you will need to provide clear and sound documentation for your selection of the employees to be terminated. And, again, federal and state laws must be followed. (Okay, for legal purposes, nothing said here should be in any way considered legal advice. I am not a lawyer, nor have I ever played one on TV.)

Here are some things to keep in mind when firing an employee for a performance issue. First of all, unless it is that single action that is cause for immediate dismissal, it should never come as a surprise to an employee. As a supervisor or manager, you should be providing regular and frequent feedback to your team members on an individual basis. There is probably a standard process in place to do this on (at least) a quarterly basis. Outside of a formal process, you should be giving feedback to your team members as the situation arises. That is, if an employee performs badly, you do not wait until the next quarterly review meeting to discuss the situation. You address the issue at the earliest opportunity. This is no different than providing positive feedback. It needs to be as immediate as the situation allows. Keep in mind that discussing an employee performance issue should always be done in private.

Again, your company policy will likely have a process to provide verbal and written warnings to your employee regarding their poor performance. A second key part of this process is a performance improvement plan. You need to clearly show the employee (in writing) how to improve upon the performance issue and correct any problems. This is also an opportunity to ensure clear communications with the employee. Ask them to explain the reason for their performance. Ask them what they feel they need to improve. Listen with patience.

A third point to keep in mind is that you are responsible to your company to ensure quality employees. It is one of your roles as you transition to a leader. You are managing company resources in a responsible manner. Managing employee performance issues is a key part of this responsibility.

When the time comes that you do need to terminate an employee, there will be guidelines from your human resources team. You need to follow these very strictly. If the situation allows and is permissible, then you may also want to provide whatever assistance is allowed in helping your employee through a transition.

I have not had to fire many employees in my career, thank goodness. It is not something any team leader looks forward to doing. In a case when I had to fire an employee for performance issues, I did everything as outlined above and under the guidelines of our human resources policies. It did not make it easy, but at least the situation was extremely well-documented. There was no misunderstanding on the employee's part because of the documentation of the performance issue.

More difficult for me was a situation when I had to fire employees as a result of a downsizing in the company. I myself had survived numerous downsizings at Sprint over the years. Having been a survivor, I hadn't given a lot of thought to the firing process. It eventually hit home, however.

I was managing my team of wireless support engineers for half the country when I was given a team of wireline technical engineers. They supported business customers for voice and data networks. This was at a time when I had transitioned into the wireless world. About this time, we had had some big cuts in our expenses. My team was scattered around the country, and I was not allowed to travel to meet the new members in person. Initial meetings were all handled over the phone.

It was a very short time later, only a matter of a couple of months, that I was told I had to let go all but one individual of the six that I had just inherited. I was not at all comfortable with the situation. I did not really know the individuals, and I had certainly not had the time to evaluate their performance. A call to their former supervisor provided very little assistance. So, I formulated a plan.

I developed a spreadsheet that encompassed the major duties of their positions. Knowing what I did about the business, I provided a weight to each item. I next added their years of experience, their train- ing and certifications with a weighting as well. Finally, I added items that identified the direction the company was taking with the type of work they did, including changes in the product mix. Again, every- thing was weighted by its level of importance.

I used their prior performance reviews for some of the information. I used their employment history and training history for some of the information. Finally, I interviewed each of them to discuss their strengths and goals. Yes, it took a lot of time to do this. With so much at stake for them, I owed them as much time as it would take within the confines of the target date that had been set for me. I rated each employee on each item and multiplied each item by the weighting fac- tor to arrive at an overall score for each individual. The top scoring individual was the one I kept. It was as fair as I could make it.

I then called each employee and explained the results. As they were aware that the cuts were coming, but not to what extent, it was not a total shock for any of them. I was very empathetic and offered any assistance as I could to help them transition. To an individual they thanked me for the manner in which I made my decision.

It was some months later that I received calls from two of the indi- viduals. They wanted to let me know that they were employed. They both went out of their way to thank me again for the manner in which I fired them! That let me know that I had done it in the right way. One of them had gone into a completely new direction with his career. He felt that losing his job was one of the best things that could have hap- pened to him.

Firing someone is difficult. You have to have some empathy even in the worst of the situations. You have to know that you did everything possible to give the employee the opportunity to be a success. There can be happy outcomes; although, you will not likely be as fortunate as I was to be made aware of them.

Now, I want to explain the heart of why I placed this topic here and not in the next chapter on the Leadership Phase. I was still in my Transition Phase when I addressed this issue for the first time … with a bit of a twist. I had an employee who had given her notice that she would be leaving the company. This was of her own volition and not a result of her performance. In fact, she was performing quite well. She was leaving because her husband had taken a promotion that would require relocation.

All was well until she let me know that their move would be delayed for several months. I had no problem with this. I had not yet conducted interviews to replace her position. My boss, however, felt quite differently.

I need to provide a little background at this point. I was in a new management position, and I was definitely in the Transition Phase. My manager was a young individual who was ready to climb the corporate ladder at any expense. He was the type who used the people who worked for him as stepping stones. He was only in his current position to look good so he could advance to the next position. He was truly not a leader. I had seen this manifest itself in meetings with him. After he was updated on key issues, he would go to our director and take personal credit for everything positive, and point to his subordinates for anything remotely negative.

Back to the story. I let him know that this particular employee would be staying on for some time. He immediately noted that she had given her notice of termination and that our human resources department had already begun the paperwork for her exit. I indicated that I could talk with the human resources manager to resolve that issue. His response to me was a huge no. He was adamant that she had given her notice and a final date of employment, and she would be leaving. Further, I better see to it that she was gone. I was shocked. But, in hindsight, I knew that he did not want to appear to be not in control of the situation.

Had I been in the Leadership Phase of my career, I would have handled this better and fought for what was right. Instead, I did as my boss told me. In effect, I now had to fire someone for basically no cause. (Up pops a red flag!) I was totally uncomfortable with this, but I had to follow my manager's directive. I told the employee what the situation was, and she was furious. I could not blame her ... but she blamed me. The next day she went to our VP and made her (very legitimate) case to stay on the job. A short time later, the VP visited my office and made it very clear to me in a very assertive manner that she would stay. My manager remained silent during this time. When the VP talked with him about the issue, my manager let me take full responsibility for everything. I had lost on all fronts with this one, but I have to tell you, it was a tremendous learning experience for me!

Obviously, this was not a firing as one normally thinks of it. But, it was a situation that made me want to address this issue in the Transition Phase. You need to handle the firing of an employee in the right way. You need to be strong and follow your convictions with integrity.

I would later need to let an employee go for performance issues. I handled it properly. But, the situation I just described was an out-of-the-ordinary circumstance that could have been handled better. You may have to face some situations in the Transition Phase that you will not handle properly. It is part of your growth process. You have to get over these things in your head, learn from them and move forward.

Temptations

How do you say no to the temptations that will take you in the wrong direction? As you grow, you are given more latitude in making decisions. That is part of this Transition Phase. With this expanded degree of independence comes an expanded degree of responsibility. You have demonstrated a degree of trust to your manager and to your co-workers. Remember also that you have had more exposure to "short-cuts" in the workplace. All of this can come together to also provide some degree of temptation. These temptations may expand throughout your career along with your expanded roles and responsibilities.

You might want to go to **Appendix 1** and take a look at **Rules 7, 8** and **9**. Let's take another look at these beginning with **Rule 7**. It's the one about adultery. As was stated in this rule, attraction to another may be fine if you are single and seeking a relationship. But, if you are married, it is a big red flag. You need to be cautious when working with others. Be careful not to mistake friendship and assistance with anything more than what it is. And, if it is turning into something more, then you must stop it, and stop it quickly.

You need to be especially careful when traveling on business. You may still be attending training or you may be in a position where you are now traveling more as you take on additional responsibilities. You are away from home, away from the office and away from the eyes of anyone that you know. You will share meals, and perhaps after-hours social events. Don't let that friendship and relaxed atmosphere lead to something that it should not. If it feels wrong, it is. If it doesn't feel wrong, it should. This is when you must reach deep into your integrity, strength and faith to maintain proper control. Some businesses avoid having members of the opposite sex travel alone together for good reason.

Let's look at **Rule 8** which has to do with stealing. We previously looked at taking pens, pencils and papers. We talked about "fudging" on expense reports or adding extra hours on time sheets, or perhaps adding billable hours to a client's bill. All of these "small" issues are stealing. With the additional latitude you have been given in your responsibilities, these temptations will grow. You will hear from others in the workplace how many of these things are okay since "everyone is doing it." Some will justify it by saying that they deserve these things since they are not paid as much as they should be.

We also looked previously at stealing time from the company by spending non-productive time on the internet for personal reasons. Any way you look at this it is stealing. Even if the company says it is okay in limited circumstances, do not do it. Avoid developing a bad habit that will only grow. It seems that bad habits tend to grow much easier than good habits. Maybe it's because they are planted in deep fertilizer, if you get my meaning. Good habits require more true nurturing.

Rule 9 is about lying. As with most temptations, these things can appear in various degrees. Misleading someone is a form of lying. This could be about a product or service you offer to your customer. It could be about the results of some analysis or testing that you have done. You may tell yourself that you are only "stretching the truth." No, you are lying. If what you are saying feels wrong, then check yourself.

Also with regard to Rule 9, we looked at taking credit for another's work. Think about how you would feel if you had completed a project or a report that took a lot of effort. Then someone comes along and takes the credit. Not so good, is it?

You have to remember that what you do has a ripple effect. There was a sales rep who had a tendency to "oversell" to the customer. He would promise more than he could deliver. Now, at the time we had a terrific team that would go out of their way to make anything work. They would get the details on the service he sold and pull out all the stops to make it work. This often took them away from other work and always took more time than should have been allowed. Resources were depleted to the deficit of other customer projects. There was often bickering among those supporting this individual, who would nearly always pledge not to do this again.

Of course, there were instances when the team could not pull off what he had sold. The team had to put a lot of effort in to trying to find a solution, but it did not always happen. He would then go back to the customer and apologize that the company or the team could not make his proposal work, thus misleading the customer and placing the company in a bad light.

This person was a top sales rep, but his technique placed the company and the team in a bad situation. He was tolerated because he was a top sales rep, but he eventually left the company. He liked to "think outside the box." The problem was that he did this in a vacuum and did not share his thoughts to get another opinion before selling the customer.

In your career, you will see others who make more money than you for doing similar work. You will be passed over for a promotion that you felt was yours. You need to be cautious in such situations with trying to make yourself look like more than you are. Rely on your firm foundation of a good Christian work ethic, and maintain your integrity at all times, especially when facing temptations. *God blesses those who patiently endure testing and temptation. Afterward they will receive the crown of life that God has promised to those who love him. And remember, when you are being tempted, do not say, "God is tempting me." God is never tempted to do wrong, and he never tempts anyone else. Temptation comes from our own desires, which entice us and drag us away* (James 1:12-14 NLT).

Regarding Worry

I previously confessed my inability to remember people's names. Of course, this is one of the key issues regarding listening. I failed. Okay, here is my next failure: I am a worrier. I have always been a worrier as far back as I can remember. Interestingly, I seem to worry more about the small things than the big things. I am sure some counseling somewhere along the way would have helped me. But, I also failed there.

Okay, enough about my failures for now. The Transition Phase is where you may experience some concerns about your career and begin to worry, if you are prone to do so. Maybe you are seeing others advance around you, feeling your skills are not being fully utilized, or maybe you experienced a first failure with a project or task. Perhaps your expanded responsibilities and freedom have overwhelmed you a bit. So, you begin to wonder if you are meeting the expectations of your management.

Jesus taught very clearly about this. Here is a simple summation. *Don't worry about anything; instead, pray about everything. Tell God what you need, and thank him for all he has done. Then you will experience God's peace, which exceeds anything we can understand. His peace will guard your hearts and minds as you live in Christ Jesus* (Philippians 4:6-7 NLT). Don't worry about anything. Okay, that has been difficult for me. I always like to tell my wife that I am only being well-prepared by analyzing all the options in every situation. That sounds like I am a good planner, but I am a worrier.

So, I decided to do something about it one day (ultimately with more success than with remembering names). I really do not recall the exact circumstances. I think it was in a conversation with one of the nuns at a parish council meeting at church one evening. At any rate, the nun, Sister Ann, organized a class to address this very issue. She was a very caring individual always thinking of the needs of others. She was one of the most truly caring people I have ever met. The timing of the class could not have been better, as I was in a position managing a data center, which is a 24/7 responsibility. Oh, I worried plenty.

Interestingly, as the class developed and we discussed the need to have quiet time with God, we entered into the topic and practice of meditation. Now, for me, non-churched most of my life and now in the Catholic Church, this idea of meditation seemed out of line with the Catholic Church. But, as we studied this expression of prayer and practiced it within the manner accorded by the church, it became an enriching form of worship for me. The Catholic Church talks about three forms of prayer: vocal prayer, meditation and contemplative prayer.

Vocal prayer is just as it says. It is a commonly practiced form of prayer where we present our love, needs and thanks to God in a verbal manner. This could be quietly within our own heads or actually out loud. In a hierarchy of prayer, meditation is next. Some practice it by reading or engaging in vocal prayer and then leading to a deep and quiet pondering upon those words. The third level in this hierarchy of prayer is contemplative prayer. Whereas in meditation we are reflecting upon the words of God, in contemplative prayer the goal is to establish a much closer relationship with God. You might think of being lost in loving God such that you are unaware of all else around you. These are my narrow interpretations of what I understand from some time ago.

So, as I developed a daily practice of meditation, I found it to be very helpful in controlling my worrying nature. Through controlled breathing techniques I was able to fully relax. I could control the relaxing of muscle groups. I could feel my heart rate lower as my breathing slowed. It was truly relaxing. Then to meditate on God's word or to just be open to his direction by listening, really listening, was actually very uplifting mentally, physically and spiritually. (Once again, the power of listening is demonstrated.)

I practiced this morning meditation most days for all of my working career. Sure, I missed days, and there were days when I could not still myself, but I did not give up or quit. I found it to be a great way to begin the day. Oh, you don't have time? You have kids to get ready for school, breakfasts to make, a spouse who needs your attention? Where would I get an hour or even 30 minutes to meditate?! And, it is a madhouse in the morning!

Well, it doesn't need to be an hour or 30 minutes. Start out with five minutes or ten minutes. Yes, get up ten or fifteen minutes earlier in the morning. Go find a quiet place; hide in the laundry room if you have to. Just spend a few minutes quietly with God. If the morning doesn't work, what about in the evening after everyone else has gone to bed. I know you are tired at this time of the day, but maybe this is just how you need to end the day. You can take as much time or as little time as possible. It can be well worth it, and I would suggest you pursue this further with some reading on the subject. Maybe your church even offers a class in Christian meditation. As usual, it takes a little effort to reap the reward.

We get some really specific direction on this in Matthew 6:6 (NLT): *But when you pray, go away by yourself, shut the door behind you, and pray to your Father in private. Then your Father, who sees everything, will reward you.* The reason why most people never hear God speak to them is that they never slow down and quietly listen. When things may seem to be falling apart, sometimes the best thing you can do is sit alone with God and wait. Instead of listening to your fears, listen for his word. Yes, this does mean giving up some of that control that you so badly desire.

I have continued my morning quiet time with God to this day. I have not substantially increased the time I spend. I have not relied on some rote words or prayer. I do begin by giving thanks for the many blessings in my life. I then simply ask for God's guidance in my day. Then I listen. Sometimes my mind wanders. I just try to still myself again. It does get easier over time. I strongly urge you to begin or renew such a practice. It has been extremely valuable to me. It may help you to control temptations and scale down your level of worry. So far, unfortunately, it has not helped me remember names.

Skill Building

There are two things I have tried to (over)emphasize. One is developing great listening skills; the other is the fact that you will always be learning throughout your career. Depending upon your background, training, career moves to date and your position, there are a few skills which you need to have a good grasp of by this time. If you are not proficient in these skills, then they could be the source for your not feeling totally at ease with yourself in the Transition Phase. By the way, what are you transitioning to? Okay, the next phase is the Leadership Phase, so it is probably evident. Yes, you are transitioning to a leader. I have already discussed the need to develop a servant's heart. This is necessary to become a solid servant-leader. But there are also certain skill-sets that you need to demonstrate as a leader.

Public Speaking. You may have been called upon by now to speak to a group in some way or other. At its simplest, you may have had to provide a project update or a weekly report on your activities in a staff meeting. This was likely done in a mostly casual atmosphere in a group with whom you have developed a degree of comfort.

Next, you may have had to provide a project update to a larger group. This may have included a more formal type of a presentation. For a good number of people, this is where it starts to get more difficult. Public speaking is a skill that every leader must develop.

Fear of public speaking is also a common phobia. It can range from slight nervousness to paralyzing fear and panic. It has been estimated that 75% of all people experience some degree of anxiety or nervousness when public speaking. In fact, surveys have shown that most people fear public speaking more than they fear death! If it helps, it has an intimidating, or maybe a humorous, name: glossophobia.

Glenn Croston writes in "The Thing We Fear More Than Death" for *Psychology Today* online, "When faced with standing up in front of a group, we break into a sweat because we are afraid of rejection. And at a primal level, the fear is so great because we are not merely afraid of being embarrassed, or judged. We are afraid of being rejected from the social group, ostracized and left to defend ourselves all on our own. We fear ostracism still so much today it seems, fearing it more than death, because not so long ago getting kicked out of the group probably really was a death sentence." It is interesting how deep the roots of this fear run.

But with preparation and persistence, you can overcome your fear. Following are nine suggestions quoted from Daniel K. Hall-Flavin in his article "How Can I Overcome My Fear of Public Speaking?" from Mayo Clinic online.

- Know your topic. The better you understand what you're talking about — and the more you care about the topic — the less likely you'll make a mistake or get off track. And if you do get lost, you'll be able to recover quickly. Take some time to consider what questions the audience may ask and have your responses ready.

- Get organized. Ahead of time, carefully plan out the information you want to present, including any props, audio or visual aids you'll use. The more organized you are, the less nervous you'll be.

- Practice, and then practice some more. Practice your complete presentation several times. Do it for a few people you're comfortable with. Ask them to give you feedback. Or, record it with a video camera and watch it so that you can see opportunities for improvement.

- Visualize your success. Imagine that your presentation will go well. Positive thoughts can help decrease some of your negativity about your social performance and relieve some anxiety.

- Do some deep breathing. This can be very calming. Take two or more deep, slow breaths before you get up to the podium and during your speech.

- Focus on your material, not on your audience. People mainly pay attention to new information — not how it's presented. They may not notice your nervousness. If audience members do notice that you're nervous, they may root for you and want your presentation to be a success.

- Don't be afraid of a moment of silence. If you lose track of what you're saying or you begin to feel nervous and your mind goes blank, it can seem like you've stopped talking for an eternity. But in reality, it's probably only a few seconds. Even if it's longer, it's likely your audience won't mind a pause to consider what you've been saying. This might be a good time to take a few slow, deep breaths.

- Recognize your success. After your speech or presentation, give yourself a pat on the back. It may not have been perfect, but chances are you're far more critical of yourself than your audience is. Everyone makes mistakes during speeches or presentations. Look at any mistakes you made as an opportunity to improve your skills.

- Get support. Join a group that offers support for people who have difficulty with public speaking. One effective resource is Toastmasters, a nonprofit organization with local chapters that focuses on training people in speaking and leadership skills.

In my own normalcy, I do have a great fear of public speaking. Here is how I fair with regard to the suggestions for handling this fear. I could do the preparation part well. In a typical business setting you will be talking about a topic you know. That should be fairly well-covered in most cases. Second is the part about getting organized. That has always been easy for me as I am a very well-organized individual (to a fault according to my wife). The third suggestion above is to practice. Unless something is sprung on you last minute, or unless you tend to procrastinate, you should have the time to practice. From there, it would pretty much fall apart for me. I could not visualize success, only failure. Breathing. Okay, not bad until I was out front. Then I had to work hard to slow down. Focus? Moments of silence? Gaaahhhh!

When I realized that I would be doing more, not fewer, presentations, I addressed the problem head-on. That is how I feel all problems need to be addressed. Face it and deal with it sooner rather than later. I looked for opportunities to get up in front of people and speak. In fact, I found a way to do this on a weekly basis. I became a lector at my church. During a Catholic service, a lector walks to the front of the church, opens a book of scripture readings and reads the assigned scriptures aloud to all those gathered. I, of course, prepared well and practiced. For weeks, then months, I would sweat just waiting to walk up the aisle. While I eventually became more comfortable, I never got over my nervousness. But, I was able to get better control over my nervousness. I actually found that, for me, it was easier speaking in front of a large group. I could let the large crowd just appear as a large mass in my mind. It took away the personal one-on-one aspect of speaking to a very small group, which for me was more intimidating.

The Toastmasters International organization also opened in our town. We met in the building where I worked, which made it very convenient to attend. It was like a next step in my process of overcoming the fear of public speaking. It was especially intimidating for me as it was typically a smaller group presentation. In addition, I knew a large number of people who attended the meetings. For me this just added to the intimidation factor, especially since one of those people was my vice-president. It was very helpful for me, and I would highly recommend this as a means to overcoming this fear if you should so need. And, even if you do not have a fear, the meetings present great opportunities to get feedback from a friendly group.

Today, I can speak in front of a group without feeling the weight of the world. I do not sweat. My mouth still gets incredibly dry in this situation, but I do enjoy speaking. I could not have done this without at least the two means I noted and without more practice than you can imagine.

Collaboration. Maybe this was something you practiced to some degree in your training prior to coming to work. But, for the most part, our education has been an individual thing. We have been taught to do our homework and pass our tests on our own. Collaboration was not allowed; rather, it was considered cheating.

Collaboration is working together to achieve a goal. It is the essence of teamwork. You have your individual specific assignments, but in some manner you must engage with others to arrive at a successful conclusion to the assigned task. It may be as simple as gathering information from someone else to add to a report. It may be as complex as working on a project team with multiple members who ultimately have a common interest in achieving success. In business you must work collaboratively; you simply cannot work in a vacuum.

If you have not practiced collaboration, it may feel foreign to you. You may feel that someone else will get credit for the work that you do. You feel as if you are relinquishing control of the situation. When others on your team do not have the same focus as you or do not see the same path as you, it can be very uncomfortable. While you may have a particular role to play, the ultimate goal is not your own personal success, but rather it is the successful outcome in achieving the group goal. I talked earlier about being a good people person. This becomes very important when working in a collaboration.

You will need to relinquish some control. This requires trust. Trust is a two-way street. You must be able to trust others to perform their part of the task and to commit to the project. You must be trustworthy by doing the same. Trust is not, however, blind trust. If you question someone or something, you will need to do your homework and establish your case. Most importantly, you cannot make the issue a personal one.

Along with trust comes respect. Someone is the team leader and deserves the respect of the group. As you work with others in a fashion of trust, you will see how respect is earned.

Communication is one of the keys to success in a collaboration. Everyone on the team must understand the status of the project at all times. As a contributing member, you must communicate your status and your concerns. Perhaps you feel strongly about some particular issue. If you are going to win over the group to your way, then you have to sell your idea with good communications. If you cannot communicate your ideas well, then no matter how good they are, others may just not see it. Again, remember to listen, especially when you have a concern.

Always distinguish facts from opinions. Decision-making must be made with facts and in a timely manner. Key issues must be resolved in order for the team to continue to move forward. Because of deadlines, timeliness of the decision process is important. Remember that others may be waiting on your decision on your part of the project before they can continue.

Realize that not all the decisions made by the team will be unanimous. You must learn to understand that a consensus must be reached in a collaboration. If your opinion is in the minority, then prepare your best argument with the facts. Once a consensus has been reached, then as part of the team, you need to accept it. This may be the most difficult thing to do in a collaborative effort.

Another very difficult part of a collaborative effort is sharing your knowledge. You may have heard the adage that "knowledge is power." You may have been placed in a particular role because you have demonstrated a particular strength and knowledge in some area. You may have a tendency to feel that this particular strength or knowledge is what gives you an edge over others. Well, give it up. You are no longer in school working for a student of the month award. You are now a responsible individual with a task at hand and a group goal to achieve. There is no reason to play things close to your vest. Use your skill and knowledge for the good of the team — for the good of others. It is no longer all about you.

Finally, recognition is important in a collaborative situation. Good work should be recognized as one means of keeping the team morale high. Caution needs to be taken not to get into a habit of rewarding every minor effort. Too much recognition for the smallest of reasons makes the reward meaningless.

Collaboration and teamwork will be important elements throughout your career. You must learn to play well with others in these cases. You do not abandon your personality, your talents or your thoughts when collaborating. Rather, it becomes a time to work on the skills required to work with others, to share knowledge, to learn and to communicate. Surely, always remember that you can never forget to rely on the basics of honesty and integrity.

Plan B. Whether working in a collaboration or alone, it never hurts to have a Plan B. What skill is this? It is about organization and planning. I emphasized these skills in the Initiation Phase. Hopefully you have practiced these skills. Well, I now want to focus on one aspect of these skills, Plan B.

Plan B means having a back-up plan. I call it good planning, my wife says I am being pessimistic. I am sure the truth lies in the balance somewhere in between. Perhaps you have given this idea some thought with regard to your career. If you do not get a position you had hoped for, then what is your Plan B? Do you continue to gain what you can from your original position, or do you shoot for another position. If you did not get that promotion, then what about a lateral move to gain experience?

Maybe more relevant to the discussion at this point is having a Plan B for a project. Good project planning calls for you to be aware of the scope of the project, the timeline, the cost, the resource requirements and communications. There are a lot of facets to a project. If you are a team leader for a project, then planning for the success of the project means being prepared for the unfortunate turns that the project will take. This is the concept of Plan B.

Being good at Plan B means a couple of things. First of all is having a Plan B. You cannot be good at it if you do not have one. The more projects you are engaged in, the more you are aware of the pitfalls that can happen. This is part of the experience you are building in your career. You should take the time to evaluate the risks of whatever you are undertaking. This should be commensurate with the scope of your work. A small project with little impact should there be a set-back will not necessarily require a great deal of planning through a risk assessment. It could be something you just keep in the back of your mind. A large project, however, may require a written risk assessment. You will take advantage of your knowledge, your understanding of the processes involved and your awareness of your team's abilities in identifying risks and preparing a plan.

When I was a project manager, Plan B was a given for every project that I ran. I created a full-blown project plan that included a risk assessment section. This was not only for myself and my team, but it was also for the customer. Most customers greatly appreciated seeing that there were contingency plans in the event of a glitch.

So, having a Plan B is the first part of the equation. Being good at Plan B is another issue. If you have given realistic thought to your Plan B, the execution of it should appear rather smooth to the project team and to the customer. I often told my team that one of the keys to success as a project manager was to never let them see you sweat. The idea is to take the bad situation, enact Plan B with a calm and cool confidence (even though you may be dying on the inside), and provide the team and the customer with a great experience. Your team and your customer will appreciate it. You will demonstrate great leadership through a tough situation. And, don't forget, now that you have enacted Plan B, there are new risks to assess and a new Plan B to consider.

Professional sports coaches do it, military leaders do it, chess masters do it ... you are in pretty good company by practicing your Plan B skills.

Technical Skills. If you are in a position utilizing specialized skills, then it is incumbent upon you to ensure that you keep your skills sharpened. You may have advanced to higher levels of a specialized skilled position. You may even be in a supervisory role. You need to maintain your skills at a level appropriate to your position requirements. For many such positions, there are specific certification requirements to attain and maintain. Hopefully your company sees the benefit to your certifications and provides some type of program to assist you in maintaining your certifications. If you are in this type of position, you understand the need to maintain your certifications, and you certainly understand that there is a real effort involved in maintaining them.

If you are not in a position requiring certifications, then there still may be reasons to pursue additional training as you attain higher levels of responsibility. Your company may provide specific formal training programs either inside or outside the company. I would suggest that you attend all that you are able to.

There are also means to obtain informal training. You may belong to a professional organization that has regular meetings that allow you to expand your skills. Perhaps you are in a position to attend trade shows where there are often free seminars on topics of interest. And, finally, you can pursue work assignments as available that will allow you to practice and improve your skills. Sometimes it will be entirely up to you to manage this type of training. You may need to take the initiative to pursue these options. This has the added benefit of displaying your interest in personally managing your career.

Even in a non-technical position, you make use of technology in your work in some way. Depending on the degree of need, you should ensure that you maintain those skills relative to your use of those technologies. If you see that the next level of advancement for you involves additional types of technologies or advancement in your current technologies, then by all means pursue the required training. You do not want to fall behind in the skills required on a regular basis to complete your work. As your company embraces new technologies, you must do the same.

Be Prepared for the Unexpected

So, you have thought about and even planned for your next position. You have prepared well for it, and you feel you are ready for that move up. You may by now also be thinking about a move outside of your area to gain a broader experience of your company's operation. This can be a good thing to do. Just remember that when you move into a new area, you will have a brief time in the Initiation and Integration Phases. You will need to learn about a new department or team. There will be new practices and processes and procedures. Hopefully, with the experience you have gained to date, the time in these first two phases will go quickly.

Sometimes this can happen unexpectedly. You may be placed in a new department or section or division by your manager so that you can gain experience. It may be a position you were not planning on pursuing in any manner whatsoever. It may be just a matter of uncontrolled circumstances. The situation may have been totally off your radar. Look at this as a great opportunity and move into it with no regrets. It is another great learning opportunity. You can only prepare for the unexpected by expecting anything and looking at everything as an opportunity. Maybe you can consider it as part of your Plan B. Plan now how you will handle such a situation.

I was managing our data center at United Telephone of Indiana. I was a manager, but I do not feel that I was yet a leader. I was close, however. Just a few years into this position, we merged with one of our sister companies. (As a side note, there is no such thing as a merger. One company will take over the other. This could result in a completely new culture to fit into.) This merger moved our data center to the other company. My job was gone. It was a circumstance totally beyond control.

My wife and I had already decided we were not going to move. This was one part of our Plan B. We had already moved a couple of times with the company. We now had children in the picture, and we liked the town where we lived as a good place to raise our family. A move was simply out of the question for us.

In the previous chapter, I talked about a particular manager I worked for. While we had diametrically opposed personal lives, I did not let that interfere with the quality and integrity of my work. He greatly appreciated my efforts. Now, years later, my job is gone, and I find out that he is looking for a data product manager. The telephone company's marketing and sales group was expanding beyond voice products and services and into data products and services. They needed someone to develop the product line.

I had no background in marketing or sales other than a minor in Business Marketing from college. Was I unsure that I could handle the position? Yes. My confidence, however, had been building over my last two positions.

Fortunately for me, the individual who I had formerly worked for knew the scope of my talents. He had confidence that I could do the job. In fact, when I asked to see a job description, he said he did not have one as this was an entirely new role in the company. I was told that I would write my own job description. (I had previously been part of a group trained in job description writing for the company, so this was easy for me.)

So, I used my IT skills and knowledge to develop this position. Having run a data center, I knew something about the needs of our potential customers. I knew the need for quality products to ensure that proper service levels were maintained. My experience was coming into play. I was able to draw upon my background to fill in the blanks. My organization and planning skills would be essential to making this work. It would also provide me the opportunity to embrace and practice presentation skills. I could see the opportunity before me to grow in those areas where I felt I was weakest. That would be a good part of your career planning. Look for those opportunities to use your strengths while growing where your skills are most lacking.

Interestingly, while this business growth would open up new opportunities to the sales team, they were not interested in learning about the data business. I developed a training class for them, but they still called on me to go on sales calls with them. Well, more opportunity for me to grow.

This story continues, but I will try to keep it short. With the success I demonstrated, I was eventually responsible for all business and residential products for the company. Not bad for a former computer programmer. Then the sister company we had "merged" with decided that all product management should be done at their location. Once again, my job disappeared. Plan B still said no more relocation.

The next move, however, was almost a given. I had developed the data products and services. I was going on sales calls. So, I took the initiative to put a plan together to develop a sales team just for data products and services. It would start out with just me to prove that this could be a successful venture, much more successful than it now was with the current sales team who was not that interested.

I became the data sales person for the state. We quickly added another sales rep, and before long I was the sales manager for a data sales team. Again, not bad for a former computer programmer. The real benefit for me was that all of this experience prepared me to move into the Leadership Phase. Being flexible and open to change was a real key for me. But, I could not have done it without faith that it would all work out for the best. Faith that when one door closes, another opens. *I can do all things through him who strengthens me* (Philippians 4:13 ISV). Through this strength I had finally found my voice, and I realized there was much more ahead for me. More surprises were to come, however.

Choose to Be Excellent

Each one of us has been blessed with particular gifts and talents. What is really significant is that we are not all blessed with the same talents. It would be a pretty bland world if we were. Sure, there are others who share similar talents in different degrees. The difference can simply be in how you choose to use your talents. How do you see yourself with regard to your talents? Do you realize that you are unique and that the manner in which you to choose to use your talents is unique?

In considering your career goals, remember that you need to spend some time assessing yourself. You should be having regular meetings with your manager to discuss your goals. At the same time, you should be performing a self-assessment. You want to compare how you see yourself with how your manager sees you.

You should always be asking yourself where you want to be in five years, in ten years. What personal development do you need in order to get there? How can you really use your strengths — your gifted talents — to get there? And, certainly assess your gifts. You may find you are developing gifts that you did not know you had. As you are provided with more challenging assignments, you may discover these formerly hidden talents.

Sometimes it is a matter of sitting down with yourself and asking what activities bring you the most joy. Yes, what really gets you energized? What makes you want to get out of bed in the morning and jump into this crazy world? Now, if it is only a great cup of coffee, then maybe you should consider a position as a barista at Starbucks®. But, go deeper. Why is it a great cup of coffee? Maybe you just enjoy making the coffee. Maybe it is a sense of completing a task, or maybe it is being creative in the type of coffee you make. At any rate, dig deep ... and hopefully, it is more than just a cup of coffee that is your joy.

So, can those things that bring you joy be channeled into the everyday challenges you face at work? How can you leverage those talents? If you are a creative person, then you might have a real gift for thinking outside the box for process or project issues. Maybe you just love facing new challenges on a daily basis. In your Transition Phase, this might be just what you need.

Of course, you need to be honest with yourself. But, you can choose to use your talents and to be the exceptional individual that you were created to be. Excellence may have certain requirements dependent upon your particular situation, but excellence is also a choice.

Leverage your strengths. Also, help your manager to better understand your strengths so she can utilize your talents to the fullest. Then, think about your weaknesses and how you can build on your strengths to overcome your weaknesses. You will find that you can develop new strengths, or even uncover talents that you did not know that you had. This can be an exciting revelation.

This to me is the core of developing your goals: knowing your talents and your weaknesses, and then building on your talents as you overcome your weaknesses. It is your choice to develop your talents and overcome your weaknesses. It can be eye-opening, and it is not necessarily easy. But remember, "No one can prevent you from choosing to be exceptional" (Sanborn 2004).

Have Some Fun!

Life is a quest. The object of that quest will change over time. You may succeed at your quest, or you may decide that you chose the wrong quest and start off on a fresh one. Of course, you can, and probably do, have many quests at any one time. You have quests at work as you pursue your career, and you have quests in your personal life as you pursue your life's desires.

You know what, though, you ought to be having a little fun on your quest. Whether your quest is a success in business, a strong marriage and family or a quest to right the wrongs of the world, you ought to be having some fun.

Having fun can be a real asset in your daily quests. Fun can help you to be creative. Sometimes lightening up a little bit can change your perspective on a problematic situation. Just a chance to look at things a little differently for a moment could make a big difference.

Fun can help you look outside the box. Think of some really wild and crazy ideas regarding your current situation with regard to making a key decision. Sometimes those can trigger a real solution that is not so crazy. Then you can experience the joy of arriving at the answer.

Fun can relieve tension. Of course, you need to be cautious about the use of this with others. In some situations, trying to inject some fun or humor can be disastrous when done at the wrong time. You really need to know the group well and read the situation carefully when trying to engage a group.

And, of course, fun can help in getting a quick recharge of your batteries. It can offer a short respite from the daily grind, maybe just enough to allow you to continue your quest with renewed energy.

A quest has the characteristics of passion, enthusiasm, appetite for life, engagement, commitment, adventure, failure, growth and determination. All these qualities exude joy! They are not limited to your personal life or to your business life. They are life-fulfilling, period. Take them with you wherever you go.

Fun and joy should be staples of life no matter what your quests are or wherever they take you. The quest itself can be difficult enough. Especially in the Transition Phase, you may have a need to renew your passion. Have some fun with it!

The Twelve Disciples

When we last looked at the twelve disciples they were still learning while traveling with Jesus. He told them of his impending suffering and death, but they did not quite get the ultimate mission for Jesus. They had even argued about which of them was the greatest. They were also now aware that the chief priests and elders were not happy with Jesus. Things were about to change for them in a big way.

The leader that he is, Jesus understands their doubts and fears. We see him address the disciples in John 14:1 (NIV): *Do not let your hearts be troubled.* He continues to tell them that he will prepare a place for them and that they know where he is going. But Thomas speaks up, perhaps expressing the thoughts of all of them, *Lord, we don't know where you are going, so how can we know the way?* (John 14:5 NIV). But, they continue to be puzzled when he explains that he is one with the Father. He eventually tells them that he will send the Holy Spirit to them after he has gone to continue to teach them. He finally tells them that they must love one another as he has loved them. And in John 16:1 (NIV) he says, *All this I have told you so that you will not fall away.* Throughout this dialogue in the Gospel of John we see two things from Jesus. He tells them how difficult things are going to be for them, then he builds them up with encouragement. He is perhaps clearer with them than he has been at any point. The disciples reply, *Now you are speaking clearly and without figures of speech* (John 16:29 NIV). A good leader is honest even when things are tough for his team. But, a good leader is also encouraging at all times. Yes, in your Transition Phase, things may seem a little empty at times. Discuss your thoughts and concerns with your manager. A good manager will give you an honest assessment of the situation and provide some encouragement for you. Sometimes just that little bit of encouragement is all you need to improve your outlook.

Now Jesus has the twelve disciples come together for a meal. While the meal is in progress, Jesus washes the feet of the disciples. It is even at this time that his betrayal and death are so imminent that Jesus continues to teach them. It is in this act that he once again teaches the concept of a servant-leader.

It is next that he explains to them that he is about to be betrayed by one of them that is sharing the meal. He tells them again that he must leave. He further tells them that they will all scatter that very night as Jesus' troubles begin. Simon Peter tells him that he will never leave him; Jesus replies by telling Simon Peter that he will deny Jesus three times before the night is over. Obviously, they are all feeling a little more puzzled and maybe just a little bit more doubtful now than they had been before. They thought they were on this long-term mission and had been well-prepared with Jesus' teachings, but now it looked like it was falling apart, or at least taking a turn they were not ready for. Could they handle the transition? Were they as prepared as Jesus told them they were?

But Jesus goes on to offer them some comfort. He says to them, *I tell you the truth, anyone who believes in me will do the same works I have done, and even greater works, because I am going to be with the Father. You can ask for anything in my name, and I will do it, so that the Son can bring glory to the Father. Yes, ask me for anything in my name, and I will do it!* (John 14:12-14 NLT). He further makes a promise to send the Holy Spirit to continue to teach them and guide them. Before offering some final prayers, Jesus lets them know that while they will be grieved by his leaving, this grief will surely turn to joy. He will see them again.

Most of us know the rest of the story. Jesus is arrested. The disciples scatter. Peter three times denies even knowing Jesus. They witness his arrest, his mock trial, his scourging and ultimately his death on the cross. They have lost the leader. Now what happens? Their company and their new careers have undergone a drastic change. They are lost as to what to do.

Three days later, the empty tomb is discovered, but they still do not understand. Then Mary Magdalene tells the disciples that she has seen Jesus, that he is truly alive. They all gather together to talk about what has happened. One of the gospels tells us that they were behind closed doors, perhaps still fearful for their own lives, when Jesus appeared to them. He explains to them that they have witnessed what had to happen; they have seen the goal of his personal mission. The Gospel of Luke tells us that he opened their minds to understand the meaning of the scriptures. He would appear to them several times subsequently, perhaps to check up on them and to encourage them in their transitional state. Other than the one who betrayed Jesus, the disciples all remained in their new careers. Shortly, they would leave the Transition Phase as they would become leaders.

Heart of the Matter

1. The Transition Phase
   - You have handled increasing responsibilities excelling in your niche
   - You have gained confidence in your abilities as you have more autonomy
   - You have grown, matured and expanded your knowledge and experience
   - Your thoughts run to advancement
   - You may feel a sense of unease about your opportunities
   - You, your situation or your company may have changed
2. You are in a service position — develop a servant's heart
3. Having a team leader, supervisor or manager title does not make you a leader
4. Hone your communications skills, especially listening
5. Learn from your mistakes
6. If it feels wrong, it is
7. Be prepared for the unexpected
8. Have some fun!

6

Expressing Your Voice
The Leadership Phase

And you yourself must be an example to them by doing good works of every kind. Let everything you do reflect the integrity and seriousness of your teaching. Teach the truth so that your teaching can't be criticized. Then those who oppose us will be ashamed and have nothing bad to say about us (Titus 2:7-8 NLT).

Depth and Breadth and Confidence

In the Transition Phase, you found your voice. You have now figured out who you are at the core, and you have been able to gain a new vision for yourself and your future. Your training, your experiences and your maturity have culminated in someone who has found a new degree of confidence that perhaps had not previously existed. Without seeing you express it openly, others recognize your confidence as well as your abilities. There is a depth and breadth of experience that has increased your value to the company. As you continue in the Leadership Phase of your career, the scope of your experience will continue to grow.

You may now be in a mid- to upper-level management position

where you are establishing operational objectives and work plans. You are delegating assignments to employees who report to you. At this level, you also develop, modify and execute company policies that affect immediate operations. You may continue to grow at this level through opportunities to broaden your scope of experience in other departments or divisions in the business.

You may be at a higher level as a director or an executive in the business. As such, you direct and control the activities of a broad functional area, usually through several departmental/functional managers. You establish and direct strategic plans and business objectives.

But, there are also those in the Leadership Phase who are not in managerial, directorial or executive positions. As was previously stated, you can be a leader without being in management. These are the subject matter experts (SMEs) who are those go-to people for the "real" answers. Not only do you have the highest level of professional skills in your area of expertise, but you have also demonstrated the communication skills and interpersonal skills to be an effective leader. While your title may not reflect that of a leadership position, your value to the business is reflective of a leader. Many SMEs make a very good salary. They will typically be called upon by the upper level positions of the company to provide input on problem resolution or strategic direction. I wanted to make this clear as the Leadership Phase is a part of your career that does not necessarily mean that you have a specific leadership title.

It becomes obvious that this career phase encompasses a gamut of roles within the company. This is where you will spend the largest share of your career. You may have changed positions numerous times, but at this point, you are very open to new opportunities and new challenges.

Someone asked me about those who are not in the Leadership Phase, but simply perform their job very well every day. I have two things to say about this group. First, they may be those unofficial leaders for their work group. Maybe they are not at the SME level, but they are still a solidly recognized resource within their team. Maybe they will grow as time goes by, or maybe they will be satisfied to remain at the level that affords them some degree of personal comfort or satisfaction. This may be their highest level of achievement within the Leadership Phase, and they are satisfied with it. Every company has these people. They are good servants in their attitude. They are mature and confident. We need these people who will serve on teams and be great team players, and in some cases unofficial team leaders.

Now the second group is considerably different. While they perform their job well every day, they are not career-minded. They do not look at their role within the company as a part of a career. These people have jobs that they enjoy performing. They go home at the end of the day feeling good about their work, but the work is nothing more than that. They are not career-minded individuals. As such, just as I noted in the Introduction, this book is not directed towards those who simply seek a paycheck and not a career.

As a career-minded individual in the Leadership Phase, you are committed to helping others establish their way and achieve success. In some way you are involved in planning and risk-taking while developing new standards or processes and employing quality in all that you do. You are providing direction with regard to strategies. Others are reaching out to you for guidance and counsel. You are an inspiration to others who look to you as an example. You help to build relationships and earn trust among others. Whether directly or indirectly, you may be involved in training and teaching others. Your thinking is more long-term and strategic in nature, and you will question existing rules, procedures and processes. In short, you have transitioned from a role as a manager to a role as a leader (regardless of your title).

At the end of the Leadership Phase you will be aware that you are achieving your ultimate career goals. And, don't forget, keep re-establishing those 1-5 year goals for yourself. Of course, you are involved in some way, depending upon your level, in establishing broader goals for larger groups, and perhaps strategic business direction. You offer a high degree of value to your organization, and they have likely invested a great deal in you in developing that value.

What I want to do at this point is organize some of my own thoughts on leadership. Yes, I have read a lot of books on the topic. And, yes, I have attended many classes and seminars on the topic. I was headed in the right direction, but all of the books and classes helped provide better focus, guidance and understanding of how to proceed. What I am sharing here are those things that I found myself emphasizing when working with my teams. Maybe more importantly, these are the actions that worked in the real world and produced great results. What great results? Highly functional and productive teams. Individuals who were never fearful to speak their minds but always did so with respect. Teams and team members who received numerous awards and kudos for their excellence. Customers who were well-served and who also recognized the team members. There are plenty of other facets to the leadership role than those I will discuss here, and I will at least try to mention some of those.

Before I move on, let me mention a couple of things that I feel are worth noting. First of all, I hope you have been guided by **The Basics (Chapter 1)**. As you move upward in the company, temptations will increase. So, now is the time to be sure you are in touch with your core of ethics and integrity. Remind yourself of this daily. You are *the* role model to a very many people now. Go back to **Chapter 1, The Basics**, or to **Appendix 1, The Ten Rules in Action in Your Career**, and place those **Ten Rules** fresh in your mind.

But for now, here are those things that were effective for me as a leader over a number of years in multiple roles with numerous teams.

Servant-Leadership

I simply cannot emphasize enough the concept of servant-leadership. Untold numbers of books have been written on leadership and servant-leadership. I will not attempt to cover the amount of material that is available through plentiful resources. This is one of those areas where you need to do your homework. In all likelihood, you have already done this. Your company has probably provided a number of opportunities for you in this regard. Do not forget that it is never too late to learn. Remember, you should always be learning. This does not change at the Leadership Phase. In fact, it may be even more important as you are the one setting the direction for others, perhaps for a large department, division, or even the entire company.

The Robert K. Greenleaf Center for Servant Leadership notes that the phrase "servant leadership" was coined by Robert K. Greenleaf in his essay *The Servant as Leader* first published in 1970. So, this is definitely not a new concept. Now, while Jesus did not use that specific term, I would say that he was certainly one of the first practitioners of the concept. But regarding Greenleaf's essay, here is what he said about this according to the Robert K. Greenleaf Center website:

"The servant-leader is servant first… It begins with the natural feeling that one wants to serve, to serve first. Then conscious choice brings one to aspire to lead. That person is sharply different from one who is leader first, perhaps because of the need to assuage an unusual power drive or to acquire material possessions…The leader-first and the servant-first are two extreme types. Between them there are shadings and blends that are part of the infinite variety of human nature.

"The difference manifests itself in the care taken by the servant-first to make sure that other people's highest priority needs are being served. The best test, and difficult to administer, is: Do those served grow as persons? Do they, while being served, become healthier, wiser, freer, more autonomous, more likely themselves to become servants? And, what is the effect on the least privileged in society? Will they benefit or at least not be further deprived?

"A servant-leader focuses primarily on the growth and well-being of people and the communities to which they belong. While traditional leadership generally involves the accumulation and exercise of power by one at the 'top of the pyramid,' servant leadership is different. The servant-leader shares power, puts the needs of others first and helps people develop and perform as highly as possible" (Greenleaf 1970).

You have to ensure that you are more centered on the needs of others than you are on your own needs. The success of your employees needs to be in the fore of your mind. One of your primary goals is to help others succeed. Your employees need to see this in action, not just in words. To this end, you need to be recognizing and praising excellence immediately when it is observed. And, you need to understand that praise and recognition is seen differently for different people. So, you need to know your people individually and treat them accordingly with recognition in a form they will truly appreciate. This includes knowing those who do not like to be openly recognized, but would prefer a personal recognition in a very personal way. Some people look for recognition from those outside the group. They are motivated by their customers recognizing their efforts. Remember, everyone has customers.

Whom Do You Serve?

When we talk about being a servant, it is fair to ask about who it is that we serve. It seems pretty obvious that in the course of our discussion, we are talking about the group or team for whom you are responsible. But, let's take just a moment to talk about just who it is that you serve.

First of all, if you are a person of faith, then it should be obvious that the first object of your attention is service to God. Since God is the Creator, what could he need from us? I think it lies in the response from Jesus when he was asked about the greatest commandment. We took a look at this in the section entitled **The 10:1 Factor in Action** in **Chapter 1** in Jesus' words from Matthew 22. He says to love God first, but he also says that just as important as this is to love your neighbor. I think this is how we serve God. We take care of our neighbor, of those in need, by conveying mercy and grace to others. It is not about judging others; it is truly about caring for others. Further, it does not matter where you find others — at home, at work or anywhere in the community — there are no limits to caring.

The next object of our servanthood is our family. If you are married you understand the importance of caring for another who is very close to you. If you have children, then you truly understand the importance of being a parent and providing unconditional love to your children. Your family is your primary focus of servanthood after God. It is with our family that it is most likely easiest to express our servanthood in a meaningful way. Yet, at the same time, if we do not have a firm foundation based on **The Basics (Chapter 1)**, we can also find that our family may be the easiest to neglect as we pursue other desires — money, glory, fame, sex, lust or control. **Rules 2** and **5** are important with regard to servanthood.

I feel that those at work fall into the next category of those we serve. Personally, I always referred to those I worked with as my work family. That is how I felt about those people I spent most of my waking hours with. And, just as with your own family, there are going to be those individuals whom you do not really like. But, like them or not, you do learn to get along with them and treat them in a civil manner. They are family after all. As you are placed in, or perhaps have unofficially assumed, a position of leadership, you have specific responsibilities to serve this group. *So Jesus called them together and said, "You know that the rulers in this world lord it over their people, and officials flaunt their authority over those under them. But among you it will be different. Whoever wants to be a leader among you must be your servant* (Mark 10:42-43 NLT). This is the concept of servant-leadership. So, while Robert K. Greenleaf may have given it a name, the concept has been around quite awhile, and it appears in most religions.

As a servant-leader, you should also keep in mind that at work you are serving others outside of your team as well. Let's take a look at two other groups whom we serve in our work family.

First, you are also a servant to your customers. Remember, we all have customers regardless of our position. We all provide a service of some type to someone. As a CEO, your customers are your entire customer base. You are ultimately responsible for the service that your business is providing to your company's customers. It is in serving your customers that your business succeeds; without customers, you have no business.

At every level of leadership, from SME to CEO, you are providing a service. As such, you have responsibilities to your customers. It is up to you to make it easy for your customers to do business with you. You must perform as promised. No, you must *out-perform* what you have promised. You must manage your customers' perceptions. Even if you are doing everything right according to your business processes, if the customer does not perceive it as such, then you must correct that. Maybe most importantly, however, is to never compromise your values, ethics, honesty and integrity. You must ultimately be accountable for your customers. Oh, and don't forget, listen to your customers. Truly listen.

Your other customer at work is your boss, whether that is a manager, director, VP, CEO or board of directors. I always felt that after I cared for my team and took care of my customers, my next order of business was my boss. I always challenged myself to make my boss look good. How better to do this than by maintaining a high-performance team and extraordinarily satisfied customers. When you give this a little thought, you will realize that with this focus you are setting yourself up for success in every way. Your boss recognizes your successful efforts. And, don't forget, if your boss gets promoted, who better to step in than another highly successful leader — *you!*

I worked for one manager on two occasions about five years apart in totally separate positions. He took a chance on me to develop a new area of business for him because I demonstrated success the previous time I had worked for him. I did a very good job for him the first time around and made him look good. I continued to do the same in the second position for him. This ultimately led to a promotion for me.

Know Your Team

Only in serving your team will you ultimately be successful in serving your customers and your boss. The key to serving your team is recognizing the talents and strengths of your team members. One critical part of this is understanding the personality of each individual. To do this you must get to know them. Obviously, if you are the CEO, you cannot personally know every employee to that degree, unless you are the CEO of a very small company. If that is the case, then do get to know all of your team. But, certainly, as CEO you will know your executive team intimately.

When I started my first job out of college with United Telephone of Indiana, one of the first people I met was the president of the company. He wanted to meet every new employee. As I was part of a newly developed fast-track management trainee program, he also met with me on several occasions during my first year to ask how the program was going for me. He was truly interested in me. He took the time to find out about me personally, and ours was not a small company. I don't know how often he did something like this with others, but he did seem to be very familiar with a large number of employees. He made time for these relationships because he knew it was important. It made me feel very good about choosing to come to work at the company, and it was not in any way superficial. My experience with him left a long-lasting impression on me. And, interestingly, when he retired, his replacement was just as personable. He ensured he left a legacy that would outlive him.

Back to recognizing talents and strengths. When you do this, you have the opportunity to place people in positions to make best use of those strengths. It is your job as a leader to understand what makes each person tick. You must capitalize on the individuality of each person. You should know how they think, how they learn, how they relate to others, how they want to be recognized and rewarded, what drives them, what challenges them, and what their personal goals are. With all of this, and more, in mind, you are able to establish an environment that allows each individual to flourish. In this way you are helping them to become the most productive employee that they can be.

At one point in my career at Sprint, I inherited two different groups to assemble into a technical support team for large wireless business customers for the eastern half of the U.S. One was a group of technical engineers, and the other was a group of customer support representatives. The engineers were obviously more technically inclined while having limited customer contact. The customer support reps, on the other hand, spent most of their time being in contact with customers, and they had a lesser degree of technical skills. What was needed for the new team was a perfect combination of the two.

Now, just about the time I was getting to know everyone and progress was being made, the objectives of our team changed. Rather than being a technical support group, we were now to be a project management team supporting implementation of new wireless services for major business customers. Having formerly managed a team of project managers, I was well aware of our goals and objectives in serving our customers, and I was able to clearly communicate this to the new team. I would need to coach them, and rather quickly, into a project management mindset. It was critical that I understand each individual so that I could help them step into this new role.

By understanding their individual personalities, I was able to assign them appropriately to meet the needs of our customers. But even further, as a team now responsible for a new way of doing business, we saw areas of great need in the company's processes and procedures for rolling out massive numbers of wireless devices. One specific area of concern was custom configuration of every wireless device to meet the customers' specific needs. To put this in perspective, we handled projects that involved rolling out from 2500 to 500,000 devices for a single business customer at multiple locations across the country.

After unsuccessfully trying to find an operational group in the company to manage the custom configuration activity, I realized we had the talents to perform this within our own team. I had a group in the southern U.S. who had the expertise and the entrepreneurial spirit to take this on. Had I not taken the time to get to know my team, I would not have been able to see this as a solution to our problem. That small group found the space we needed, obtained the hardware and software that would be required, and established a process to meet the requirements on a nationwide basis. They were the right people to make this work, I knew they had the capabilities, and maybe more importantly, I knew they had the right spirit. This was the type of challenge that got these individuals out of bed every morning. Only because I knew them individually was I able to convince others that we could do this, and do it very well. By tapping into their strengths, I was able to expand their productivity level allowing them to accomplish more than many thought possible.

Here's another example of knowing each individual on your team. I had a good, steady individual managing a project for a customer. The project had gotten a little sideways, and the customer wanted the project manager replaced. I spoke to the customer to get to the root of the problem. (Listen to your customers!) The customer simply felt that the project manager was not taking enough control. In the background, I knew that he was; however, because he was trying not to stress out about the situation in front of the customer, the customer perceived that he was not in control. It was truly a matter of perception, but perception is the truth to the customer.

They wanted a take-charge individual. So, knowing my team, I was able to quickly assign another project manager who I knew would meet their specific requirements. No time was lost in making the transition. The customer appreciated this, and they were well-pleased with the new project manager.

The story does not end here. The original project manager was less experienced than his replacement. He was not doing a bad job; he had just not read the customer well and adapted to their needs. I did not just toss him aside. Instead, I had him sit in silently on every customer conference call so that he could learn how to recognize the individuality of the customer and how to work with this type of customer. I knew, based on his personality, that he would benefit from this. As is best, this turned out well for everyone. The customer was happy. The original project manager truly took this as a learning opportunity. And, the replacement project manager was able to use his skill-sets to benefit both the customer and the company while helping to teach a fellow employee.

My team developed into strong project managers once provided with appropriate project management training. We were serving some of the corporation's largest business customers with great success. Knowing each individual allowed me a great deal of flexibility in making assignments, monitoring our activities and celebrating our successes. Each of them discovered more about themselves, faced challenges head-on, became more focused on critical issues, and grew tremendously both as individuals and as a team. They were well on their way to becoming leaders.

Know What You Don't Know

As you broaden your base of knowledge of your business, you will at some point be leading a team who has skill-sets that you do not. Perhaps you have moved from an accounting leadership position into an operational leadership position. Maybe it was specifically to expand your base of knowledge, or maybe it was because that particular functional area needed someone with your strengths to resolve some process issue. Whatever the case, you are now leading a team whose skill-sets are outside of yours. It may seem daunting at first, depending upon your confidence in your leadership skills. You have to realize that you could not do the work that your team members perform on a daily basis. It is okay to admit this to yourself.

Is it okay to admit this weakness to your team? I say that you surely better! You cannot fake anything with your team. You need to let them know that you are not in a position of leadership in order to perform their work. You are there because you are a leader. Then, you need to explain how you lead and what you will do for your team in general. That is, let them know that you will do everything you can to make it easier for them to do their jobs to the greatest degree of success. Let me be very clear, this should not be confused with trying to make their specific jobs easier. You will do everything that you can to break down any barriers that get in the way of their ability to be successful. This includes evaluating processes and procedures, ensuring proper training and providing the right tools.

Then, you listen to your team. They may not open up right away. Some might even feel that you are setting them up to see how they respond and weed out the troublemakers. If their previous manager was not a good leader, you will face this type of caution from them. You must build a bridge of trust with them. This may take some time. But, continually listen. Whenever you have the opportunity to make even the smallest helpful change, do it.

I had been a project manager at Sprint for implementation of business customer voice, data and video solutions. I later managed a team of such project managers. Using my background and knowledge of project management processes, I helped develop new standards for this team. Then, through a reorganization I was given a team of wireless systems engineers to manage. I had absolutely no wireless background … other than owning a wireless phone. I was now the leader of a team of wireless technical engineers.

In our introductions to one another, I let them know of my background. I let them know my areas of experience and success. I then proceeded to let them know that there was no way I could possibly perform the work that they were doing. But, I did let them know that this was not my purpose. I told them I wanted to make their jobs easier to perform. I wanted to tear down their roadblocks and ensure they had all the tools they needed. And, I wanted them all to be successful.

At the same time, I did not simply dismiss the fact that I could not do their jobs. I asked each of them to take a little time with me whenever we had an issue to discuss and provide me with a little more detail on the technical side of the matter. I asked lots of questions, and I listened a lot. I made it clear through my actions, and not just my words, that I was really interested in understanding their needs and their concerns. They came to the realization that I did care about them and about how they performed their work. They saw that I would do everything in my power that I could to make them more productive. Over time I was able to break down barriers, improve processes and communications, and establish a foundation of mutual trust.

There is a side to this that you need to be aware of. As a leader you cannot say yes to everything just because you are trying to make your team more productive. There will be those who will test you and try to take advantage of you. When called for, you need to be a disciplinarian. I helped my teams to understand that discipline is not about rules and bureaucracy, but rather it is about responsibility and freedom. When individuals are disciplined in their work, they earn the freedom to take control over situations, to make decisions on their own, to earn rewards and to learn from their mistakes.

You should be respected as a leader, but you must show that there is reason to respect you. In the same manner, you can respect each individual, but they must earn that respect as well. Your words must be clear, understandable and strong while also being empathetic. You must always be aware and committed. Your powers of persuasion must be strong as you influence the near-term to improve the long-term. Your communication skills have never been more important.

Tear Down Roadblocks

In my first position in the Leadership Phase of my career, I was a sales manager for a team selling data and video network solutions to our business customers. There were a few other leaders who shared common views of how to build successful teams. There was a manager whose team consisted of technical engineers who designed the solutions for the customers. There was a manager over the field technicians who installed the solutions. We were all innovative and entrepreneurial in nature. Our general directive was to grow our non-regulated business. You need to keep in mind that at this time the telephone companies were highly regulated by the government and had only relatively recently been given more latitude in our non-regulated business ventures. As managers, we made a group decision to run our teams like this was our own business. We took ownership. We maintained full responsibility for our actions and our results.

As a management team, we decided to do whatever it took to successfully grow the non-regulated business in an ethical way. We talked about how to best utilize our resources. Being the organizer that I am, I developed a model of how we could do this. First, I had been working on setting up my sales team by market segment. Thus, this became the basis of the model. We then placed functions over this model. A functional team would support each market segment. Each segment was assigned a sales rep, a sales support engineer, installation techs and a logistics rep. Each team was to be coached by one of the managers. With the limited resources available, some individuals, including the managers, were supporting two teams.

Did we ever break down roadblocks! Our general manager worked with the accounting department to make changes that allowed us to better track our profitability by market segment. He was also able to convince the accounting department to make changes to the accounting procedure that allocated certain costs from the regulated side of the business to our non-regulated business. This helped to improve our overall profitability.

In my role, I defined the markets and developed tools to help us better understand each market so that we had a better grasp on selling to the customers' specific market needs. I also developed a full business plan for the unofficial organization. The manager of the field technicians was able to re-badge the service vehicles to place an emphasis on our business offerings. The manager of the sales engineers began supporting new products and services with additional training through our suppliers.

We were breaking down roadblocks all over the place. We were being leaders. We were moving way too fast for some people, but it was coming together with great success. We had a local VP who strongly supported our efforts. We had regular team meetings with him. A typical meeting might involve a clerk explaining to the VP why we needed to make a change to our ordering process. He listened, and he followed through.

Then the sister company with whom we had merged (that is, they took us over), decided to make some structural changes to the organization as they consolidated management roles. Each of us was now reporting to different managers, some of whom were located remotely in Ohio. Those particular managers we reported to were "dated" in their perspective on leadership. (I think I am being kind in stating it in this manner.)

My particular manager in the Ohio company who had taken over me and my team was not happy ... until he saw our sales results. He was better after that, but he was still not entirely sold on our plan for managing our business. It was simply too far outside the box for his old-school management style.

We, however, continued moving forward and after quite some time of great success, we saw that we needed additional resources to continue to grow the business further. I revised our business plan, and we appealed to the VP in Ohio for a meeting to listen to our business case. Unfortunately, my boss in Ohio wanted nothing of it. It was beyond his comprehension that someone as far below a VP as each of us was could meet with and discuss business plans with a VP. He was another roadblock to overcome.

Having broken down the barriers, we had our meeting in Ohio. The VPs listened intently and nodded their heads approvingly. At the end of the presentation they announced their pleasure with what we had put together. It looked good to them ... and they would get back to us. Not good. With my sales experience, I was well aware that we had not closed the sale.

Our plan was not approved. That, however, did not deter us from continuing to manage the business with our market-focused teams. I have never been involved in knocking down so many roadblocks to the benefit of the team and the business. It was one of the most exciting times for me as a leader. I will come back to this story later, however, as there is more.

Ensure Training

Your team needs to keep their skills sharp no matter their type of work. It may be anything from technical training requiring certification and re-certification to leadership training. Whatever the role of your team, they need to stay current in order to be most effective and most productive. Some of the training will be common to every team member; for example, achieving certifications. Other training should be as needed for the specific individual. This, once again, requires you to understand not only the strengths and weaknesses of each individual, but also their personal career goals. You may have a well-performing technical employee who desires to move into management. After discussing her future and assessing her readiness, you can help establish the course of training required for her to succeed at her future goals. A leader needs to be looking out not only for the team's near-term successes, but also for their future personal successes as individuals. Despite how much you may depend upon someone in their current position, if they have a desire to move up, you need to do all you can to support them. If they are not ready, you need to honestly let them know why. You then need to be able to coach them in how to overcome their shortcomings.

On the other hand, if you have someone who is quite competent in their position and their desire in life is to continue in this type of work, then you need to support them as well. Their training may be specific to their role, but it may also include training in presentation skills or communications skills as needed. They may be those SMEs who will be functional leaders. If, however, your team is used as a developmental area that trains employees and moves them on, then the story is different. You need to coach them through this position and determine where their next step will take them.

Recognize and Reward Your Team

Everyone desires to be recognized for their efforts in some manner. But not everyone desires to be recognized in the same way. Some businesses have recognition programs. I have seen good ones, and I have seen bad ones. Let's take a look at a bad one.

Each of the managers was asked by our VP to recognize and reward one of our employees for excellence at our monthly operations meeting. That is a good thing. Recognition in front of your peers is typically viewed as positive by most of us (although, not by all people). Well, this program started out good. After recognizing a few people on my team over a few months, I was ready to recognize an individual for a second time for an effort that was above and beyond expectations for a special project. But, I was told I could not do this. I had to recognize someone who had not already been recognized. What?!

A recognition/reward program has a two-fold purpose. First, we want to reward excellent performance in an individual (or, perhaps, an entire team). This is to be encouraging and supportive of the individual or team being rewarded. It is positive reinforcement to encourage continuing such behavior. The second purpose is to provide encouragement to others to pursue excellence in their own performance.

Suddenly, I was not allowed to reward what was the best performance on my team for that particular month. No, I had to select someone else ... I guess so no one's feelings would be hurt. Good grief. This sort of sounds like the "everyone is a winner" model being espoused in many schools. We cannot recognize and reward sub-par performance, or for that matter, even expected performance. If you have an employee who feels bad about not receiving a reward, then there are other problems to work on.

The other complication with this program is the idea of a monthly award. What if I did not have anyone with what I felt was an excellent performance worth recognizing in the past month? Was I to lower the standard just to recognize someone? The answer is to deliver a monthly reward only when there is a performance worth recognizing. In other words, this topic would be a regular part of the monthly meeting, but it would not be required. Rather, ask if there is anyone to recognize and reward. Only recognize and reward outstanding performance. Do not lower the bar. In this manner the reward can be something special for a truly outstanding performance, not merely a small token that must be handed out every month to meet some program standard. In this way, an employee can have a real sense of achievement when being recognized and rewarded.

No Compromise

Your team will be no better than your personal worst (that is for *you*, the leader). Hopefully, you have a team that is completely ethical and has their integrity intact. At some point in your career, however, you will have people who will test you. They may push you, or they may simply wait and watch to see what you allow. They will assume that if it is okay for you to compromise your integrity in some situation, then it is okay for them. The door will have been opened, and you must now be responsible to close it. It is not a good situation.

You cannot let your guard down. You need to set the ground rules up-front with your team. Let them know that there is no compromise when it comes to ethics and integrity. In fact, go further and ensure they have training in these areas. Many companies provide this as a matter of their standards anymore. If your company does not, then pursue training outside the company.

I was confronted with an ethical situation when I was a sales manager. I am getting back to the story from the earlier discussion in the section **Tear Down Roadblocks**. Assuming you read that section, I left the story with my upper management not approving our team's business plan to grow our data and video non-regulated communications business. My manager was not happy that we had approached and had a meeting with his VP.

It wasn't long after this that this same boss came to me with a way to improve our sales numbers for the remainder of the year. I listened, of course. To keep things in perspective, I want to again point to the issue regarding the government regulation of the telecommunications industry. While the business was still highly regulated, we were opening up the non-regulated side of the business. The objective for our sales team was to grow this non-regulated side of the business. Services such as data communications circuits were still within the regulated business. In fact, they were regulated to the extent that if your business was in our franchised territory, you had to buy your circuit from us. Period. You had no choice. When a circuit crossed franchises, there were methods in place to share revenues among the circuit providers; i.e., the telephone companies.

Now, my manager wanted me to claim these regulated circuit sales as part of my team's revenue. Not only that, but he wanted us to claim five years worth of revenue for that circuit at the time it was purchased. It so happened that as these circuits were ordered, the orders were printed on a local printer for engineering and accounting.

He told me his plan. They would print an extra copy of each order. I would take these orders daily and simply distribute the copies of the orders to my sales team. They would calculate the revenue for five years and add it to their reported sales. Wow, sales from thin air!

So, I explained to him that these were regulated dollars, and our objective was to grow the non-regulated business. To him it did not matter; a data service was a data service. When this argument did not work with him, I told him that this was totally unethical as my sales team had absolutely nothing to do with these sales, except in the case where a customer was adding a circuit as a part of our proposed solution for them. But, even then, the customer had no option to purchase the circuit elsewhere. I finally had to tell him that I just refused to do this.

Unfortunately, he was relentless. We argued over and over on this issue. He ultimately made it very clear that I would do what he wanted. But, I was not going to proceed without putting everything in writing.

One issue we discussed at length was our sales objectives. I told him that with his plan we would far exceed our sales quotas for the year. He assured me that this was a good thing, that we would all benefit. He tried his best to play me by saying that we all wanted the sales team to be successful, and that it was ultimately good for the business. I knew, however, that he was mostly interested in making himself look good. I placed my concerns in an email and particularly noted the regulated versus non-regulated issue and the effect of this on our sales quotas.

I felt terrible every time I took those circuit orders off the printer and distributed them. In fact, I did not even give them to the sales team. They went straight to the sales support team who kept the sales records. I had compromised, and I felt it.

I saw our revenues grow quite rapidly. What was I to do if a customer canceled an order? Nothing. It would all "average out" according to my manager.

So, year-end came. Bonuses based on sales quotas were good for the team, and for me they were quite good. It felt like blood money, but I was not going to turn it down.

Then, my manager came to me with the bad news. My bonus was too large. It would not "look right" to pay a sales manager a larger bonus than some directors would be receiving. I guess I should have said fine and walked away from the blood money. But, now it was the principle of the thing. I was angry. He had forced me into an unethical situation, and now he had lied to me. I decided to fight for my bonus. I discussed the situation with our VP. After some time, he told me I would be paid, but it would be a reduced amount since my quota should have been adjusted when we started the program. I had tried to get that done from the outset, but my manager had said the quotas would not be changed. I had mentioned this in the email I had prepared at the start of all of this.

So, I put together the details of the entire situation for the VP so he could see how it had played out. Ultimately, he resolved to ensure I was paid over a three-month period so that there would be no single large payout to garner attention. It should be kept in mind that while this was a very nice bonus by the standards of the telecommunications industry, I was not by any means getting rich. The biggest concern was how it would look to others in the company.

I had let my boss push me to the point where I had compromised my ethics. I was not happy with him, nor was I happy with myself. I turned in my resignation. It was a difficult situation that I prayed about. I wasn't sure it was the right thing to do, but I had to do it. I had already seen a few people leave the company because of the mismanagement that was taking place. I was next.

Here's the final part of the story. I felt a great sense of relief when I submitted my resignation. I gave the standard two-week's notice. Shortly thereafter, I received a call from the VP, the same one who had approved my payout. He wanted me to stay on for several more months to help with a transition that would be made to bring the voice and data sales teams together under a single manager. I expressed my concerns about putting the two teams together, but I agreed to stay on and help with the transition. It was an odd situation to say the least, but since I had no other immediate plans, it was fine by me. It would give me more time to decide what I was going to do next. If you have read the **Preface**, then you also know the rest of the story.

Leading a Process

As I have mentioned, a leader may not always be in a management position with a team. A subject matter expert (SME) could be an individual who is an unofficial and respected leader in an organization. But, even without a team of your own, your actions have an effect on others such that you should be a servant-leader in every aspect of the term. Everything we have talked about regarding servant leadership still applies. A twist to this is one who is in a position to manage a process, perhaps with no direct reports.

I had demonstrated my skills as a quality team leader through successful teams and projects. With recognition of my abilities, my manager brought a new challenge to me. It was to be a huge undertaking, one I would be working on solo. While not really a SME, I would be using the expertise I had honed in planning, organizing and executing. You see, I had been tapped many times to take on under-performing areas and bring new life to them. I was about to get one of my biggest challenges.

Business customer installations all across the country at Sprint relied not only on our own installation teams, but also on subcontractors who performed the work on our behalf. Over time, the number of contractors had grown to somewhere in excess of 400 companies performing installations for our business customers. The situation had been so poorly managed that the actual number of contractors was not known. My research turned up between 400 and 700 possible companies. There was no uniformity to the contracts for these contracting companies; that is, if contracts even existed. Pricing was all over the place, and there were no written standards for anything. The challenge placed before me was to clean up the mess, standardize contracts and pricing, develop quality standards and implement a method to measure successful outcomes. All of this was also to be done while paring the number of contractors down to 25 who could handle our installations nationwide.

It would be just me and my planning, organization and execution skills to handle this. I had no team, yet I had to manage a project that would involve many areas of the company. Not long after I started the project, I was able to bring on one additional person to work with me.

It wasn't until after I accepted the challenge that I learned that the individual who had been running the program before me had been fired when he could not clean it up. That made me a bit uncomfortable, but I liked the challenge.

This assignment was going to test every bit of my leadership skills as I had to lead a project involving numerous departments within the company while having no authority over any of them. I had to work with the legal department to break existing contracts and establish a single new standard contract. I had to work with the accountants on pricing models and strategies. Our logistics teams had to be engaged regarding sourcing and delivery of equipment to non-company entities. I developed and distributed an RFI (Request for Information) and eventually an RFP (Request for Proposal) to contractors to solicit input to the process. Boundaries and bidding processes were developed with every Sprint regional installation group across the country. There was a tremendous amount of detail that was a high priority for me, but just another request to those in so many other departments.

Well, I eventually had a new standard contract finalized with the legal department. I developed a very thorough and complete set of contractor guidelines and standard nationwide contractor rates. In the final selection of contractors, I brought the candidate companies together and presented our plan in great detail. It was made clear that these were Sprint standards that they would be expected to follow to the letter. I also laid out the process for rating the quality of their work and measuring their success.

This entire process took about a year. I used every facet of leadership skill that I had. Communication and collaboration were huge in this endeavor. Planning and organizing were critical. When it was done, we had 25 nationwide contractors who agreed to all the terms. The outcome would prove to save the money that this undertaking had intended to from the start.

This tested me as much as anything I have done. Having previously run my own business made a big difference for me. I had learned to rely on my skills, intuition and confidence. This challenge greatly expanded the breadth of my knowledge within the company. I stayed with the program for two years before turning it over to the other individual I had brought on board. We were recognized and rewarded for excellence in leadership for the success of the program.

The point of this was to let you know that good leadership skills are important even though you may not be in charge of a single employee. I was fortunate enough to have worked as a project manager along the way in my career. This was one of those positions with a lot of responsibility with no direct reports. The leadership skills developed in that position were very transferable in this case. My background up to this point had provided me many of the tools I needed to accept this challenge.

Sometimes you have to gather ad hoc resources to accomplish your business goals. Others can recognize when they are working with someone who has the interpersonal skills necessary to convince them to want to provide assistance. This is another one of those things that you cannot fake. If you honestly care about people, it shows. Since you have no authority over those resources, your leadership skills will be the only thing that you can rely on as you seek the support of others.

Perfection Versus Excellence

I think it is important to talk about the distinction between the two objectives of perfection and excellence. It is essential to you as a servant-leader to understand the difference. Let's first go to *Merriam-Webster* for definitions. Perfection is "something that cannot be improved." It is "free from all flaws or defects." Perfection implies that "whatever has been achieved is unsurpassable." Excellence is something that is of "extremely high quality." It is "the quality of being outstanding and extremely good." I think the differences are quite obvious.

We cannot be perfect. Period. You cannot, therefore, expect others, especially your team members, to be perfect. From a biblical perspective, perfection means to be perfect in Christ. We cannot achieve perfection ourselves, and certainly not on earth. We often strive to be perfect in the eyes of others, thus making an idol of perfection (recall **Rule 1** and **Rule 2**).

We will not be perfect in this life. Our lives are a process as we walk with Christ. So, we pursue Christ during our time on earth that we may have perfection one day in the next life.

Now, excellence, on the other hand, is something we can achieve, something we should strive for, and something we can expect of our team members. It needs to start with The Basics (Chapter 1), in pursuit of excellence in ethics and integrity. It has to be a part of your make-up as a servant-leader. Excellence in your heart will flow into excellence in all areas of your life. *Whatever you do, work at it with all your heart, as working for the Lord, not for human masters* (Colossians 3:23 NIV).

Your team should know that you expect excellence in their efforts. Excellent results should be recognized and rewarded. You also need to understand that your team is not perfect. To expect perfection in any individual or team is to simply set them up for failure. There is no perfect resolution or result. Some may see certain situations or results as "unsurpassable," but in truth they are seeing that which is of "extremely high quality."

There will be times when you will be required to make a key decision without having all the information that you feel is needed to make a good decision. In fact, you are going to find that in most such situations, you will not have all the information. Most of the time, to get enough information to be 100% sure of your decision is simply not feasible.

I was in a position at one time in my career that was highly volatile and fast-moving. I learned a lesson from my director at the time. He told me that I could not take the time needed to be any more than 80% sure in making a key decision. That was a little unnerving to me as a young manager, but I learned over time that it was an effective standard. If you think about it, 80% odds are pretty good. It is just too costly in many ways to try to achieve 100% (perfection) in your decision. As a leader, you must sometimes lean heavily on your gut instinct. Will you be wrong sometimes? Yes. If you are in an environment where this concept is understood and encouraged, then an occasional wrong decision will not be a disaster as long as you use it as a learning opportunity. Now, okay, as with any rule there are exceptions. You need to be smart enough to understand this. If you are on the team launching a man to the moon, then 80% is not likely going to work. For the most part, I am referring to management decisions.

Be firm and fair in your pursuit of excellence. Do not set up yourself or your team for failure by pursuing perfection.

Handling Failure

I think one of the things that defines you as in the Leadership Phase is how you handle failure. No one wants to fail at anything, but we all do fail. It is unfortunate that we see so much of the everybody-is-a-winner thinking in our society today. Young people need to learn how to handle failure. They cannot do this without failing. Not everyone is a winner all the time.

Many companies have a culture that has a tolerance for failure. This is especially evident in some of the premier technology companies. These companies thrive on innovation, so they must allow for failure. But what about your average business company? This is where you need to learn the culture of the company. You also need to know what the expectations of your specific management allows. It is going to take a clear understanding that comes from good communications.

And, communication can be a big part of how failure is seen by your management. If there is a huge failure with a major business undertaking, one might ask why it took so long to see the problem. A problem should not be allowed to go unchecked to the point that it has devastating effects. With good communications, problems should be identified and resolved early. Projects that are scrapped entirely are less costly to everyone involved, as well as to the business, if they are terminated earlier rather than later. Good communications can ensure that bad news is handled frankly and dealt with quickly to the benefit of all.

So, I am really going to help you out here and give you **Ten Ways that You Can Avoid Experiencing Failure**. These are nearly always certain to assure that failure is extremely minimal if not entirely eliminated! Here we go:

10. Play it safe, always.
9. Never change careers.

8. Do not try to right wrongs.
7. Do not try to sell a new idea.
6. Do not set goals for yourself or your team.
5. Do not try to help a failing employee.
4. Strive to never exceed the minimum requirements.
3. Never be innovative or entrepreneurial.
2. Never follow your dreams.
1. Stay in bed in the morning, pull the blankets up over your face and think happy thoughts.

There you are. Ten surefire ways to avoid failure! Okay, but if you want to be a success, then you are going to take the actions that this list indicates that you should avoid. Here's the hard truth, if you are going to have a successful career, then you will experience failure. You can count on it.

One of the things you should watch for is that you are failing at the right things. If you are an accountant trying to perform brain surgery, then you are failing at the wrong thing. While that is an extreme example, it is something to be aware of. Perhaps you have tried to take on a task that you are simply not prepared to handle. It is okay to admit that you are not prepared. If it is an area that you need to pursue, then get the training required. Is it a goal of yours? Did you jump into this too quickly? While you do need stretch goals that challenge your abilities, they should be reasonable. And remember, stretching is a process that takes a little time.

The key matter, however, with regard to failure is in how you handle it afterward. I like the advice given by Susan Tardanico, founding partner and CEO of Authentic Leadership Alliance, in an article she wrote for *Forbes* entitled "Five Ways to Make Peace with Failure." Here is my summary of her points:

1. You simply cannot take failure personally. Failure does not define who you are. You need to retain your self-confidence.
2. Take the time to analyze the failure. You need to get to the root

cause of the failure and make adjustments as needed going forward.

3. Stop thinking about it. Once you have analyzed it, let it go. You cannot change what happened; you can only move forward.

4. We have a fear of failure based on how we think others may view us as a result. Sure, others matter, but this is your life. Know your heart and maintain your focus.

5. Look at things differently. Get out of the negativity trap, and into a positive approach to a new solution. Take a completely different perspective on the issue, and maintain a healthy attitude.

If you are in a position that requires you to be innovative and entrepreneurial, then you better be able to practice those five means of making peace with failure. If you are a true entrepreneur, then you already do this. It is built into who you are. Think of some of the biggest names you know of in business and technology, the real entrepreneurs, past or present. They have also had some of the biggest failures. Their failures were their motivators to do more. They did not give up.

Many of the great figures of Scripture experienced failure at one time or another, yet those failures did not keep them from effective service for God. Though they failed at some point, and often in significant ways, they not only recovered from their failure, but they used it as a tool of growth — they learned from their failure. To fail from time to time is only human, but to be "a failure" is when we are defeated by failure, refusing to rise and try again. Christians sometimes believe they should be immune to failure by virtue of their relationship with God, but the truth is that God often allows us to fail for a variety of reasons, most certainly to teach us. *We are hard pressed on every side, but not crushed; perplexed, but not in despair; persecuted, but not abandoned; struck down, but not destroyed* (2 Corinthians 4:8-9 NIV). Maybe you had your first opportunity to lead, and it did not go well. Examine the situation and understand what occurred. Discuss it with your manager.

Listen and learn. Then, calm yourself, use your training and your experience, remember **The Basics (Chapter 1)**, make peace with your failure and move forward with a servant's heart.

You cannot let fear of failure paralyze you. I mentioned the concept of making decisions with only 80% of the required information in the previous section, **Perfection Versus Excellence**. This was difficult for me to do. Once I realized, however, that I was part of a culture that allowed mistakes to be made, then it became easier. It saved a lot of time and aided in moving business along at a quicker pace. Quite frankly, I found 80% to be a very good figure over the long run. The time and effort required to obtain that additional 20% of information for a "sure" decision was just not worth the effort. And, this is coming from an organized, and get-all-facts type of an individual.

Leaving

In the Transition Phase, I talked about the uncomfortable feelings you might be having about your job. You may have been at that point where you were not sure your skills were being utilized, you were not advancing fast enough or you were under-appreciated to the point that you wondered if you had made the wrong decision about coming to work for this company. I suggested you think long and hard at that time about your situation.

Maybe you stuck it out and things improved for you as you moved ahead into the Leadership Phase. Now as a leader, you have greater responsibilities to yourself, to your team and to your company. With this responsibility and your greater level of experience, you are more aware of what is being done right and what is being done wrong in your company. Perhaps changes in structure, new ownership or a new CEO has prompted a totally new direction and new culture. Recall the situation I faced in the discussion in the section on **No Compromise**. I had let myself compromise my integrity because of a manager who lacked good management skills and lacked integrity. Ultimately, I decided what was best for me was to leave the company.

One of the most important things I did when I left Sprint was to leave with good relationships. While my experience with my manager was not good, I did not use this as an excuse to bad-mouth the company. How could I when I felt I had made a bad decision. You do not want to burn any bridges behind you. You may think it is a good time to let the SOBs have it. Does it really accomplish anything? Now, you may likely have an exit interview. It is a good time to have a frank and honest discussion about your experience with the company, but it does not need to be personal. (Again, there are exceptions. A specific example might be the case of sexual harassment.)

In my particular case, just short of five years later, I sought re-employment with Sprint. Everything about my work history was common knowledge to those with whom I interviewed. Not only was I re-hired, but I was also able to have my previous service time with the company bridged. This was a huge asset to me with regard to company benefits. I had given up and felt I was at a dead-end five years prior. I was now able to return to a new group with much better management using new skills I had developed while running my own business.

With very few exceptions, there is no reason not to leave your company with a good relationship. Even if you were "down-sized" out of the company, you need to leave with no hard feelings. Yes, this can be a tremendous blow to your ego. How do you recover? Can you see one door closing and another door opening? Maybe God is leading you to a better place that he has planned for you. Maybe it is a good time to reevaluate your gifts and talents. Maybe you will get a better understanding of yourself. Again, there are tools to assist you. But always keep in mind that there may be a point in time when the business has experienced a rebound, and you have an opportunity to return. You never want to limit your options by severing relationships to the point of no return. You simply do not know what the future may hold. Remember to expect the unexpected, and handle it positively.

The Apostles

The inner core of Jesus' disciples very officially entered the Leadership Phase when they became apostles. Let's take a look at the meaning of apostle as we did with the meaning of disciple. According to *Merriam-Webster*, in the broadest sense of the word an apostle is "one sent on a mission." In the stricter sense of the word, apostle is one of those from Jesus' inner circle who were entrusted to spread the message of Jesus throughout the world. Let's check out how this happened.

The Gospel of John informs us that Jesus had appeared to the disciples three times after he had risen from his tomb. While the disciples did not recognize him at first, Jesus did reveal himself to them. The disciples had, in fact, been frightened by his presence.

They were frightened not only by the fact of his presence, but also by fact that someone had located them. The Gospel of John also tells us that the disciples were behind locked doors when Jesus appeared. At this point, the disciples were still in fear of their own safety from the Jewish leaders. We are told in the Gospel of Luke, however, that Jesus opened their minds so that they could understand the Scriptures. He went on to let them know that they had been the witnesses to every-thing that occurred during his time with them. He is now beginning to let them see that they have become the leaders who will carry on his teachings. He provides them with additional encouragement by letting them know that he will send them the Holy Spirit.

The Gospel of John relates a conversation between Peter and Jesus in which Jesus obtains Peter's commitment to be the leader of the young church. So, Jesus has begun to establish the organization and leadership for the continuation of his teachings. The disciples become apostles when Jesus gathers them together and gives them their new mission statement in the Gospel of Matthew. *Then Jesus came to them and said, "All authority in heaven and on earth has been given to me. Therefore go and make disciples of all nations, baptizing them in the name of the Father and of the Son and of the Holy Spirit, and teaching them to obey everything I have commanded you. And surely I am with you always, to the very end of the age"* (Matthew 28:18-20 NIV). They have become the apostles, those leaders who would spread the message to the whole world.

You may or may not see a clear point in time when you become a leader. As with so many facets of personal development, these things are often evolutionary in nature rather than revolutionary. We tend to grow into these things. Sometimes it becomes difficult to pinpoint the moment since it is transitional in nature. You might understand it through your actions and reactions to situations rather than as a specific job or title.

Here is my personal experience. I had been leading a product marketing team for 3-4 years. I was doing well and making some good decisions. I felt like I was preparing myself for bigger things with the passage of time, and I had that itch to be something more. For the most part, however, I was still being directed by my manager to a greater degree than I was being directed by my own ideas on how to accomplish goals and achieve the expected results. Sure I had input to those goals, but how to proceed in accomplishing them was not entirely of my own accord.

When this position was then taken away by the Ohio company with whom we had merged, and I would not relocate, it tipped me over into a leadership mindset.

I have already related the story of my development of a data sales team for the Indiana company. I had become a leader with my own ideas, goals and path to success. In developing the sales team, I had become a servant-leader. I had learned through experience how a high-performance team could operate, and I was committed to the success of everyone on this new team that I was responsible for. No one told me I was a leader. My confidence had developed over time. It was almost as if I could see how all of my past experience had come together, and I had been placed at this point in time to serve a purpose that was greater than myself.

Now, back to the apostles now in the Leadership Phase. After Jesus ascends into heaven, the apostles under the leadership of Peter elect another apostle to replace Judas Iscariot. Peter makes it clear that a replacement has to be one of the men who has been with them the entire time from the baptism by John up to Jesus' ascension. This is one of the key criteria for an apostle, he had to have known the living Jesus. This is why we as individuals can be followers of the way of Christ and even disciples, but there can be no new apostles.

The story continues in the Book of Acts when the apostles are gathered and receive the Holy Spirit, just as promised. This was a transformational experience for them. We now see the apostles kick into full gear as they begin to follow their mission. They even develop a strategy on how to carry out their mission. We see that they have changed from the fearful group hidden in a locked room to real leaders ready to pursue their mission with a clear plan that they developed. "They always went first to the great cities located on the trade routes. From these centers their disciples and converts then traveled out to the towns beyond and established still others. The apostles knew the secret of strategic locations and of delegating responsibility to others, thus multiplying themselves more rapidly than in the case of many modern missionary enterprises" (McBirnie 2004, p, xxii). The Book of Acts provides a good insight into the worship of this early church covering about 35 years.

For some time it appears that many of the apostles spent most of their time in and around Jerusalem. There may have been some hesitancy to expand beyond the Jewish nation and into the Gentile nations. Perhaps it was finally at Peter's encouragement that they decided on a world strategy of evangelism and set forth on their journeys throughout the world.

We ultimately see the apostles travel east into India where Thomas founds the Christian church in that country. Thomas apparently had a large role in establishing the Eastern Christian Church. Tradition holds that he was martyred in India having been pierced by a lance. We find, in fact, that all of the original apostles are martyred. Only Paul, sort of self-appointed but accepted as an apostle since Jesus had appeared to him after the resurrection, would live to die a natural death.

The apostles certainly fulfilled their mission to reach the world. Andrew goes into areas of Russia. We see Thaddaeus/Jude travel south-west into Saudi Arabia. Simon visits North Africa. A number of the apostles travel throughout Greece, Syria, Turkey, Iraq and Iran. Some traditions have James and Peter in Spain, Peter and Philip in France, and Peter even traveling as far north as Great Britain (McBirnie 2004).

They took their mission seriously. They developed a strategy and carried it out with careful planning. They led the young church as they were convinced to do so by their former leader, Jesus. Looking at Christianity worldwide today, no one could argue the success of their mission.

Interestingly, other than what is found in the Book of Acts and some histories from their contemporaries, not a lot is known about many of the apostles. But, think about it; they were servant-leaders. They were carrying out their mission, and always with the good of others at the forefront. They did not see any point in writing about themselves. Their service to others was bigger than themselves.

Heart of the Matter

1. The Leadership Phase
   - You know who you are at the core
   - You are committed to helping others achieve success
   - You are involved in planning and risk-taking
   - You develop standards and strategic direction
   - You build relationships and trust
   - Your thinking is more long-term
   - You continue to grow and seek opportunities to broaden your scope
2. Servant-leadership is about the growth and well-being of people, not the exercise of power
3. Tear down roadblocks
4. Recognize and reward your team — there is a right way and a wrong way
5. You will be tested — do not compromise your integrity
6. Leading a process requires every bit of your leadership skill
7. Understand the difference between perfection and excellence
8. Learn how to handle failure

7

Leaving It Better
The Legacy Phase

Therefore, I will always remind you about these things — even though you already know them and are standing firm in the truth you have been taught. And it is only right that I should keep on reminding you as long as I live. For our Lord Jesus Christ has shown me that I must soon leave this earthly life, so I will work hard to make sure you always remember these things after I am gone (2 Peter 1:12-15 NLT).

The Culmination

Everything that has been discussed up to now culminates here. As a quality leader, you have excelled in many areas including communications, planning, fiscal responsibility, culture building, strategic development and overall leadership. You are now preparing for the end of your career, or perhaps the beginning of a new part-time or full-time career. You have time to reflect on your accomplishments throughout your career as you prepare a transition plan for someone to step into your position and as you establish your retirement goals. I stated earlier that you will know when you are in this phase. It may sound a little strange, but it is true. I was leading a team that was probably one of the best I had ever worked with. I had handled some very tough situations in my career, and this team, too, had evolved through some difficult circumstances. Things were now going very well for my team and for me. This was no different than working through the other challenging times I had faced in my career. I enjoyed the challenges and I enjoyed the people, but I was truly ready to move on ... not to a new position, but to a new phase of my life.

My thoughts did not turn to coasting and taking it easy. On the contrary, I continued to do everything I could to ensure continual improvement in all aspects of the business that I could affect. All was going very well for me, but at the same time, I knew it was time for me to move on. And it was not about moving on to a new challenge and a new team within the business; rather, it was about moving on to do those things that were personally important to me. Yes, age had a bit to do with it. I was still relatively young at age 58, and my health was good. My wife and I discussed our financial situation with our financial planner. We could do this. I was ready, and I felt my team was at a point where they were ready. By this I mean that I felt that I had instilled in them the principles and discipline that would allow them to continue to succeed both as individuals and as a team. I could leave with no regrets about their situation or mine. It was important to me to leave when things were going very well. I did not want to leave problems behind me.

In those moments of reflection you are thinking about your legacy, as I did without really realizing that this was what I was doing. Legacy is about sharing what you have learned and leaving the mark of your values. When you begin to live your legacy, your influence comes from who you truly are at the core. And just when did you begin to live your legacy? It was when you began to realize who you were at that core and began to influence others for *their* success. It was in the Leadership Phase of your career. Yes, all the while you were being a servant-leader, you were building your legacy. To leave a legacy, you had to live that legacy every day of your career. You had to practice and take to heart those Ten Rules. You had to listen and be humble and build up others.

You had to take decisive actions and break down roadblocks and be both firm and empathetic. You really had to get it right from the very start at that time when you had no clue that you would one day leave a legacy.

So, while you may be thinking about your legacy at this time, and that is natural, you will come to realize that your legacy is not something you suddenly decide to do at the end of your career. You have lived your legacy daily. I call this the Legacy Phase because it is now in the forefront of your mind as you make a conscious decision to bring your career to an end. Reflection on your successes will tell you what you are leaving behind. It is a culmination of what you did in the Leadership Phase at every step of the way that becomes your legacy. It is my hope that in understanding the five phases of your career, you will become the best leader that you can be by practicing those good skills and living by those core principles that build your legacy on a daily basis.

A Human Need

Leaving a legacy is a real human need. It is part of a desire to have some part of us live on, past our retirement from our career and past the end of our lives. We want to feel like we mattered, like we made a difference. If we leave something of ourselves behind in others — through our values, ideas, teachings — we feel as though we have passed on a part of who we are. As an adult, most typically, we think of the influence we have on our children and grandchildren. We do the same thing, however, for our work family.

We don't think about this so much when we are young. We are living within the circumstances we have been placed in and making the best of it. We perhaps have college loans to repay or a young family to care for or personal relationships we are building. As we mature, we come to realize that we have a full range of choices and a freedom to make those choices no matter the experience and maturity we have at the time. We look to others for direction and course correction. With good guidance, we develop a core based on sound principles. Progressing, we eventually have the opportunity to share our body of knowledge and experience with others to the point where we become leaders.

As leaders we come to understand the importance of sharing and giving to others. We feel we have something that is good that we can put into the hearts, heads and hands of others. The choices we make early in our careers will set us on a course, good or bad. Even if we have chosen the wrong course, we still have the opportunity for correction. Often it is in making that correction (learning from our mistakes and failures) that we become a stronger and better person.

So, in the Legacy Phase you begin to reflect upon those choices, those course corrections and those opportunities you had to influence others. Maybe you did not give this a lot of thought along the way. Knowing now, however, that your Legacy Phase will arrive one day, perhaps you want to spend more time reflecting on who you are going to be in your Leadership Phase. I like the way Susan V. Bosak, educator, author and co-founder of The Legacy Project, put it in one of her guides on the organization's website: "Legacy is about life and living. It's about learning from the past, living in the present, and building for the future." I do not think you can live your career with your legacy in mind. That is a very self-centered consideration of legacy. Rather, it is by giving yourself to others as a servant-leader that you will develop a legacy. It really is about living.

So, you see, your legacy does not begin at the end of your career. It may be then that you finally give it some thought. It is the time when you can prepare a final legacy, take some final fundamental actions. But your real legacy is the sum total of your career, especially what you did in the Leadership Phase. It is how you lived your life in service, or not, to others.

It is not arrogant to want to leave a legacy. If you followed the Ten Rules in your career and maintained your integrity, gave of yourself in service to others, practiced patience and humility, understood your purpose and were focused, innovative and action-oriented, then you will leave a legacy of truth that will live on in others. By not seeking glory for yourself, you served others. By being humble, you helped others to grow stronger. By being strong, you helped others to learn self-control. By obeying a larger calling, you truly cared for other people.

While the business may judge your legacy based on organizations, buildings, systems, processes, or on the business results you achieved, the truly lasting legacy we leave is in people. Especially to the younger people at work, an older successful individual in a position of responsibility is someone they look to as an example for inspiration. This is a good reason to consider becoming a mentor in the Leadership Phase or in the Legacy Phase of your career. We leave our values in those we have the opportunity to influence through both our words and our actions.

Notice how so much of this is about how you treat other people. You see, while coaching your team — a single team, a large division, or the entire company — you were instrumental in the growth of each and every individual you touched. Your focus on making others successful has made your business decisions successful. It is successful people who make a successful business.

What's Next

What's next is what you think about in the Legacy Phase. Probably one of the most common things heard in this regard is the idea of travel. Many people look forward to traveling around the country or around the world. This can take many forms depending upon your financial position and your desires. Certainly, if your are married this is one of those things that must be agreed upon. If you plan to travel and your spouse plans to stay home and be involved in other activities, your dream could quickly vanish. These are discussions that need to take place well before your last day on the job.

Some people plan to continue working. This can also take a variety of forms. Some look forward to part-time work, either in the same industry or in an entirely new field. Some will look to perform volunteer work in a field of interest to them. There are also those who have a hobby that they have enjoyed and now want to turn that into their work.

Hobbies are, of course, a large source of pleasure for many retirees. This was the vision that I had for my retirement. So, here are some examples of how this worked for me that may be helpful to you. First of all, I have always had a great interest in genealogy. I had worked on my family history many years earlier, but this was too time-consuming to keep up with while raising a family and working too many hours. One of the first things I did upon retirement was work on my family history. My endeavors in this area resulted in a book I wrote on my family history from its beginnings in 1786. As much as anything I enjoyed the research aspect of this pursuit.

Well, I also love writing, so completing a book on my family was fulfilling. In my research I uncovered a very interesting family member. This led me on an adventure into his life that was extremely rewarding and resulted in a biography that I wrote. Oh yeah, writing is one of my other hobbies.

I have also always enjoyed photography. I never got deeply enough into it to get into darkroom work, however. Besides, I am colorblind which creates its own challenges with regard to photography. However, I love black and white photography. With the advent of the digital darkroom, I have been filled to overflowing with satisfaction with this hobby. I did have thoughts of developing this into a part-time business. I even had one paid photo shoot; however, I found that working as a photographer is very time-consuming and not nearly as satisfying as just photographing those things that I enjoy.

Finally, the most gratifying and loving activity for me has been time spent with our grandchildren. My wife has always been so much better at being engaged with kids' activities than I; after all, she had been director of a preschool for a good share of her career. Me, well I had spent more time than I should have working, which took away from time with the family. Don't get me wrong, I did not ignore my family;

we had plenty of good times and I coached my kids' soccer teams. With our grandchildren, there is nothing standing in the way of time to spend with them, and I have been blessed with every second of that time that I have.

Maybe all you want to do is go fishing every day. Simply don't allow yourself to get bored. There are so very many opportunities to be engaged with something that suits your personality, has some meaning for you, fits into your financial situation or is simply very enjoyable. Use the Legacy Phase of your career to give this some thought, and if you are married, be sure that you and your spouse are on the same page!

About the Money

If your career took you to the highest levels of the business — an owner, a CEO or any other high-level executive position — then your thoughts on legacy may include how to handle some large amounts of money you have accumulated. Perhaps you gave this some thought before finding yourself in the Legacy Phase. Prior to this time, you may already have had some opportunities to do some good things with the money you have been blessed to earn.

Hopefully, you have remained grounded in **The Basics (Chapter 1)** through the pinnacle of your career. It may actually have been more difficult to stay grounded as you reached the upper levels of the organization. The distractions are greater and the temptations can be larger and more frequent. With the great responsibilities you have had at this level, you may have found it difficult to remain true to the good person that you developed into while managing your career with sound God-based principles. But if you have stayed grounded, then you know the good feeling that it is to have served others and to have succeeded as a servant-leader, and not as one who used others as stepping stones to the top.

You likely have an untold number of stories of individuals who influenced you along the way. And, you likely have untold stories of individuals who have accomplished great things while in your employ.

So, back to the money. If you have followed the faith-based principles in your career, then you have likely done your part for your community by giving to charities and perhaps by sponsoring programs that supported your community. You have also likely taken care of your family and assured that your children have been provided the opportunity to attend college. You have probably had more than enough when it comes to money, and you have tried to set a good example for others in your use of it.

In the Legacy Phase, there are many ways to use this gift as a means to make some long-term difference for others. One consideration is establishing scholarships. There are many ways that a scholarship program could be established.

First, there are merit-based scholarships that reflect a student's abilities and may also look at the individual's community involvement. These are nice general scholarship that obviously award the work that the student has performed. The idea is to support these types of efforts as an encouragement to future success. These can be wide open, or they can be limited to specific types of study.

Next are student-specific scholarships. These scholarships target a specific group that could be defined by anything from gender to race to medical needs, and any other group that the donor would like to target.

Third as a consideration are college-specific scholarships. Perhaps your business has a specific type of an employee who is served by a specific type of college. Some examples might be nursing or education. You could fund a scholarship for a particular school or schools that provide the education for those types of jobs.

Finally, you might want to consider a career-specific scholarship. This is an option that you can nicely tie-in to your own business. An accounting firm could sponsor scholarships to accounting students. An architectural firm could target students who pursue an architectural career. You get the idea. This type of scholarship can really serve nicely as a legacy scholarship.

In a similar manner, you could also consider establishing a private, non-profit foundation. This could be used to address anything from a personal interest you have in some area of need in your community to a global need anywhere in the world. As with a scholarship, this could be specific to your business in the need that it addresses. But, it could just as easily be a foundation to support some need that is simply of personal and philanthropic interest to you and your family.

If you have been so blessed and are so inclined, I am sure you can develop many ideas on ways that you can serve your legacy through your monetary blessings either locally to your community or in some other broad manner. Your blessings can have a great lasting effect if you have the means and the motive to pursue such a thing. *Tell them to use their money to do good. They should be rich in good works and generous to those in need, always being ready to share with others* (1 Timothy 6:18 NLT).

Finish Strong

A key element to your Legacy Phase is to finish strong. If you are fortunate, you are leaving on a positive note with the company. If you are not leaving on good terms for some reason, it is not the time to spoil your career of successes with complaints or petty grievances. Don't give in to some weakness that will only leave a bad lasting impression. While your legacy has developed over years, a poorly handled exit will be the only thing that some people will remember. (Now, really, if you have been following the recommendations and performing to high levels, this should not even be an issue for you.)

No, now is the time to work on your transition plan. Work closely with someone who is slotted to take over your position. Why would you not? Hopefully, you have been preparing someone, or maybe several people, all along. This may not always be the person who is selected, but at least you can do your best to be their champion.

Also, look for any lasting fundamental changes that you may have the opportunity to make. You can actively seek out challenges and problems in processes or people and take the actions that you know will create a lasting success. You may not be around to see the final success or get any credit for it. That should be fine with you at this point. If you can make things better for others, then do it. You probably have that desire to leave things better. You probably have actually already done so, but you will likely seek some one last thing to tackle to that end.

Finally, prepare your goals. What? You say you are retiring, so what goals? Yes, you should have goals for retirement. Maybe you plan to continue to work. Maybe you would like to pursue an opportunity to serve in new ways. Maybe you will do volunteer work. Perhaps you have hobbies that you have set aside that you can now pursue. It might be the case that you are entrepreneurial to the point of starting a business of your own. Maybe you are going to travel. Whatever the case may be, you do have goals for this next phase of your life. You should not exit the business and say to yourself, "Now what do I do?" You should have a plan. You will be much happier if you have given this some thought beforehand.

The Apostles

I think the apostles thought very little about their personal legacies. They knew their mission was much bigger than themselves. They also knew of their impending martyrdom. In fact, all except John would die a martyr's death by stoning or crucifixion or one of many other horrible means. John, however, lived in exile on the island of Patmos and was the last apostle to die, perhaps somewhere around 100 A.D. Just as in our own early years as leaders, our legacy is not something we think of.

However, I do think they thought about the legacy of their roles as apostles to evangelize the world. It was their mission that defined their legacy, and it was in succeeding in that mission that they would leave a legacy for the world. In one sense their very mission was to leave a legacy. To affect the whole world with the good news brought through Jesus is a lasting legacy.

Their work in fulfilling this mission was obviously very difficult work. They likely knew that their jobs were meant to carry them to the very end of their lives. They had no thoughts of retirement. Rather, their legacy was their work, and their work was their legacy.

You will find people like this in the business world. They simply cannot imagine retiring. Their work is their legacy. Some do not handle this well, losing friends and family as they devote their lives to work. There are those, however, who have a more healthy outlook. Although their work is their legacy, they still maintain a balance in life that allows for relationships. Following those ten foundational rules is critical in achieving a balance in life that allows for this.

I think the apostles were of the group who devoted their lives to their work yet still managed to maintain some balance. We know that some of the apostles had families, and they certainly had one another to reach out to for support. They relied on each other. They relied on the new disciples that they gained in their work. They developed and maintained relationships as they remained leaders to the very end.

The apostles certainly met all the characteristics of having been in the Legacy Phase. They had most obviously left the their mark on others not only by teaching but also by living true to their core values. Others were greatly influenced by their actions as servant-leaders. The sum total of their careers as apostles was goodness given to others, hope for a better future for all believers and a young, fast-growing church founded on Christ. They were making things better for others even though they would not be around to see the fruits of their labors. They all finished strong accepting their fates to the end. Christians, and non-Christians alike, around the world today, nearly 2000 years later, still benefit from their legacies.

Heart of the Matter

1. The Legacy Phase
    • You are preparing for the end of your career, or for a new career
    • Reflection on your successes reveals what you are leaving behind
    • You have lived your legacy throughout your career
    • Legacy is about sharing what you have learned and leaving your mark
2. Leaving a legacy is a real human need
3. Learn from the past, live in the present, build for the future
4. Plan for your next phase of life
5. Understand your legacy regarding money
6. Finish strong!

Epilogue

I know that there is nothing better for people than to be happy and to do good while they live (Ecclesiastes 3:12 NIV).

As I developed the **The 5-Phase Career Model**, I kept in mind the gifts that we have each been given and the responsibility we each have in using our gifts. The ultimate gift, of course, was the life that Christ gave to free you and me from our sin. How will we use our lives in response to this great gift? Your career is one place where you will have to answer that question. It may not be the most important setting in which to answer, as your relationship with God and your family should come first. But, we do spend so many of our waking hours in the work-place that we must give it due attention.

I hope this book has been able to help you to see that there is a method by which you can manage your career. Knowing the phase you are in may help alleviate some concerns you have about your career development. Sometimes simply knowing that you are not alone and not odd because of the way you are feeling can be freeing.

Remember, *you* are in charge of managing your career. Yes, you will have bosses and circumstances that will seem limiting. It is up to you to work through those things and sometimes make decisions that may not be very comfortable. I shared with you a few of my own uncomfortable situations. In everything, you must have hope.

When you attain that position where you are responsible for others, you must have faith to get you through some of the tough times. Some days it will seem as the only place you can turn is to your faith in God.

Along the way, if you are guided by the love of Christ, you will treat people in the proper manner. Remember, sometimes that love means taking an action that may make that other person very upset with you. As long as your actions are guided by love and not by vengeance, you will serve well. Yes, let faith, hope and love be your compass.

I appeal to you to be shepherds of the flock that God gave you and to take care of it willingly, as God wants you to, and not unwillingly. Do your work, not for mere pay, but from a real desire to serve. Do not try to rule over those who have been put in your care, but be examples to the flock. And when the Chief Shepherd appears, you will receive the glorious crown which will never lose its brightness.

In the same way you younger people must submit yourselves to your elders. And all of you must put on the apron of humility, to serve one another; for the scripture says, "God resists the proud, but shows favor to the humble." Humble yourselves, then, under God's mighty hand, so that he will lift you up in his own good time. Leave all your worries with him, because he cares for you (1 Peter 5:2-7 GNT).

Appendices

Appendix 1 - The Ten Rules in Action
in Your Career

Rule 1: Honor God
- He has blessed you with your gifts and talents, unique among all others
- Ask for his help
- Listen to him

Rule 2: Do not devote yourself to idols
- Money, glory, fame, sex, lust and control, just to name a few
- Have a trusted friend you can talk with if you find yourself in trouble
- Of course, pray

Rule 3: Respect God
- Do not misuse his name
- Control your anger
- Work on your relationship with God

Rule 4: Take at least one day each week away from your job
- You need to recharge your batteries
- Focus on the other very important things in your life
- Honor God

Rule 5: Respect your parents
- As well as others in your life who have provided guidance and taught you respect
- Remember your roots
- Be your best

Rule 6: Honor life itself

- Of course, do not commit murder
- But also control any anger you may have
- Forgive

Rule 7: Honor god's gift of sex

- This is to be reserved only for your spouse
- Do not let your eyes and your heart wander
- Respect the opposite sex

Rule 8: Do not take what does not belong to you

- Work supplies do not belong to you
- Watch your expense reports
- Do not steal time from your employer

Rule 9: Tell the truth — always

- You can't take the credit for someone else's work
- You can't cover up problems with your company's products and services
- Do not mislead your customer by "stretching the truth"

Rule 10: Focus on *your blessings*, not on what others have

- You are not entitled to anything
- Life is not fair; business is not fair
- Develop yourself; build on your strengths and overcome your weaknesses

Appendix 2 – Personal Career

I have included a look at my personal career for two reasons. First, I want to let you know that I have had a very successful business career. I put in the effort at every turn to ensure honesty, integrity and quality. I failed at times, but I picked myself up, learned from the circumstances and moved forward. I utilized the experiences gained every step of the way. I had to face some roadblocks and did so by being creative and entrepreneurial. I managed my career as best I could even when it tried to manage me. It has been the experience of a broad career that has given me the expertise and knowledge to write on this topic of career management.

The second reason is to provide you with an example of one way in which a career can proceed. It isn't always straight lines and a progression of promotions to higher levels. There were several times when I took a lateral move to increase the depth and breadth of my experience and ultimately increase my overall value to the company. While most of this was within one company, this is still applicable when changing companies. Sometimes it may be good to take a lateral move even if it is to a different company to build your base of knowledge and experience in order to set yourself up for the next step upward. And, finally, sometimes your best laid plans are disrupted. Broadening your skills and being flexible are very important to managing your career.

I graduated from Ball State University in Muncie, Indiana, in 1971 with a double major in Mathematics and Computer Science and with a minor in Business Marketing. I was a student-athlete with a full-ride scholarship as a football player. I was a a three-year letter winner and a two-year starting offensive guard.

My class was one of the first to graduate with the Computer Science degree at Ball State. During our studies, a group of us approached our computer science professors recommending some business-oriented studies for computer science majors. Not all of us had plans to become hardcore computer scientists. There were many of us interested in a business career. We expressed our desire to establish a process that would allow for joint projects with the Business College. They were open to our ideas, and such courses were formed. For my part, I was able to secure a part-time job in the university's Bureau of Business Research my senior year where I was able to get some practical experience mining data from United States Census records.

I accepted a computer programmer position with United Telephone Company of Indiana upon graduation from college. At the time there were 18 local United Telephone companies across the United States. We were all part of the parent company, United Telecommunications, Inc., located in Overland Park, Kansas. As part of a new company effort to bring in college graduates, I was also part of a fast-track management trainee program at the company. I had entered the Initiation Phase of my career journey.

I moved through the various iterations of programmer, programmer/analyst and systems analyst as I progressed in my technical career. I took over key responsibilities for our toll processing systems and the labor reporting portion of our accounting system. I implemented new documentation standards and practices for the programming team. I was also responsible for establishing structured programming standards for new program development. Time and experience placed me into the Integration Phase during this time, about 1972-1973.

With greater experience and responsibility I found myself moving into the Transition Phase of my career about 1974-1975. I felt boxed in by the status of those in positions above me who had no plans to move on. I ultimately pursued an opportunity outside Indiana at our Florida Regional Data Center in Fort Myers, Florida, in 1975. It was a larger company with, in my eyes, greater opportunities for advancement.

My wife and I were not happy living in Florida, and I was able to return to United Telephone of Indiana in late 1977. I continued in a systems analyst role, but I was still feeling that I needed to expand my opportunities. Still early in the Transition Phase, I felt its strong grip on me. I still felt limited by the make-up of the IT team.

Not long after returning to the Indiana company, I took my first managerial position in the company's network department in 1979. While I had a management title, I did not initially have any employees reporting to me. I was responsible for developing and implementing several new mini-computer systems that were used to monitor our statewide telecommunications network. Within a couple of years, I had a team working for me who traveled the state to implement special network studies with portable gear that was installed at local telephone central offices.

As I approached the end of my time in this position, I also had a small staff of computer programmers as well as a computer operations staff. I had built a small network data center and eventually implemented our company's first 911 computer operations center as part of a forward-looking team.

The experience in the network department had been very good for me. I then saw an opportunity opening in the IT department. It looked like there might finally be a chance for advancement in the mainstream IT organization. I was still in the **Transition Phase**, and I decided to make another career move and pursue this position.

Building upon my experience in the network department at United Telephone of Indiana, I took over the main IT operations for the company as Information Services Manager in 1984. The biggest challenge set before me was to improve customer relations within the company. I established new practices and procedures for problem management and change management. I also established the first help desk within the corporation. I brought in some very noticeable improvements while at the same time saving money for the operation.

While I was continuing to grow, this position was not an easy one for me. I had to take over a team who had not had a lot of attention from a management perspective. In addition, since this was a 24/7 operation, it was difficult to let go of my work at the end of the day. While my experience was broadening and I was utilizing newly developed management skills, I cannot yet say that I was in the **Leadership Phase**; I was still in the **Transition Phase** of my career.

In the mid-1980s, United Telecommunications, our parent company, became engaged with General Telephone in partnering in the long distance business. The off-shoot of this was the eventual purchase of Sprint by United Telecommunications. Shortly thereafter, the United Telephone companies became Sprint Corporation. As part of a cost-savings measure, some of the statewide operating companies were merged. The Indiana company was "merged" with the Ohio company. I have used quotes because this was more of a takeover by the larger company in Ohio. We were now part of the Northeast Region which consisted of the companies of Indiana, Ohio, Pennsylvania and New Jersey. The result for me was that in 1987 all of the IT operations were moved to Ohio, which meant my position was gone. I talk about expecting the unexpected in the book, and this is a good example.

One of the managers I had worked for when I directed the computers and staff in the network department was looking for someone to fill a new position of Data Product Manager. With my IT background, I thought I would be a good fit. It worked out well as I was given the opportunity to define my own job in 1987. I developed a complete line of data products and services for the sales team. My full responsibilities included market research, product research/selection, pricing, training, sales support and process development.

I had left the mainstream IT work altogether. I was once again entering the **Initiation Phase**. Given my background and the nature of this new position, this phase passed quickly. I seemed to also integrate into the role well and also passed quickly through the **Integration Phase**.

Since the sales team's background was in selling business telephone systems, I also developed and delivered a very specific data sales training program for them. Unfortunately, none of them really embraced data sales. As a result, I spent a lot of time on sales calls with them to develop customer solutions and close the sales. I was always willing to learn.

According to my performance reviews, my management skills were improving. My department director sent me a personal note thanking me for my contributions and noting that I was catching people's attention (in a good way). I was beginning to feel my confidence developing. I was comfortable but moving into the **Transition Phase** once again.

With my success in developing data products and services, I also took over the voice products and services. Eventually this led to my assumption of responsibilities for all business and residential product and service development for the company as the Marketing Development Manager in 1988. I now had a staff of product managers and marketing analysts working for me. Revenue growth was the key goal achieved with great success.

I may have felt at this time that I was entering the **Leadership Phase** as I had grown my role and developed a team. However, in hindsight, I was not quite there yet. I can see now that I was developing a servant-leadership style, but I can also see that I was not yet into a mode where I was willing to take the risks that a good leader sometimes needs to take in supporting their position and their team.

Did I mention that you should expect the unexpected? (Yeah, I did.) I was so successful at what I had developed, that the management team for the Northeast Region in Ohio decided that this position should now be moved to Ohio. Once again, my wife and I decided against moving our family. So, in 1990 I proposed a new position to my manager. Since the voice sales team was still dragging its feet on selling data products and services, I suggested that I take over the data sales. After all, I was already doing this for the most part. So, I became a Major Account Manager consulting with customers on data communications requirements, recommending business telecommunications solutions and ensuring customer satisfaction.

Back to the **Initiation Phase**. Again, however, I passed quickly through the **Initiation**, **Integration** and **Transition Phases**. I was using my own ideas to develop my role, and I had a vision of how this could be fully developed into a larger part of the organization. My manager noted in reviewing my performance that I demonstrated outstanding abilities to change with priorities and a commitment to excellence as a core of my character.

My role as Major Account Manager proved successful enough that additional major account managers were added for data sales in 1992. As Sales Manager—Data Communications, I was given responsibility for this team which grew to six covering the state. I developed business plans for the team, set sales goals and strategies, and provided marketing support. I was now firmly in the **Leadership Phase** of my career.

I was fortunate enough to work with other forward-looking managers who supported engineering and implementation of our solutions. With a very supportive manager of our own, we developed integrated teams focused on targeted markets. In reviewing my performance, my general manager gave me the highest possible rating for communications skills with a specific nod to my team approach in managing. He also noted my growing confidence, something I could also feel. Observation was also made of my personal effectiveness and the discipline I displayed in pursuit of my goals.

All was going very well until I was placed under a new manager ... one in Ohio. His management style lacked any teamwork and entrepreneurial spirit. We did not get along. He asked me to take advantage of a flaw in the system and take credit for orders of circuits that were fully regulated and required no sales effort whatsoever. After months of fighting him, I settled after putting the entire plan on paper with all of its flaws, as well as the eventual cost to the company in sales team bonuses. I knew this was wrong, I had told him so, and I documented it with his full knowledge.

We blew our sales numbers out of the water, as I had predicted to him. He thought this was great ... until it came time to payout bonuses. I had to go to the vice president to explain the situation and fight for the bonuses for me and my team. It was a very difficult time for me, and I decided to leave the company. More unexpected change.

In 1994 after months of trying to determine my direction for the future, I left Sprint and became one of four partners in a start-up company called The NetComm Group, Inc. We were a network integration firm focusing on business/technology integration solutions for voice, data and video communications. We provided consulting, network design services, and sales and implementation of our solutions. With our major focus on community banks, we served customers in Indiana, Michigan, Kentucky and Illinois. There was very little time spent in the Initiation, Integration and Transition Phases. I already knew all but one of the partners, and we all shared a lot in common. The biggest adjustment for me was in working for myself. The Leadership Phase had to be entered into very quickly, and it was.

My personal role at the company was Vice President—Marketing. In addition to marketing duties such as developing all marketing materials and our business website, I also performed client business process reviews, account management, vendor management and project management. I had additionally developed a unique business/technology integration plan which we used for consulting purposes.

In June of 1997, we were selected by *Entrepreneur* magazine and Dun & Bradstreet as one of the 100 hottest new small businesses in America. We were number 60 on the list.

Being a small business owner is everything you might expect. It was fun and exciting, it was frightening at times and it was a lot of hard work. I worked out of an office at home, and it was just way too easy to begin my day as soon as my feet hit the floor in the morning, usually quite early. And, it was too convenient to stop in my office in the evening. I did learn that working for yourself from a home office takes a lot of discipline, and in my case this meant discipline not to overwork. I spent two days a week in our business office that was about two-and-a-half hours away. So, I was gone at least one night every week, but it was usually more than that if there were customers to meet.

Unfortunately, after nearly five years, I was burning out and had to make a change. This was very difficult for me as I very much enjoyed the people I worked with. One of the real bonuses for me was bringing one of my sons into the business. He gained a lot of good experience that served him well in his own career. It was about 2011 when the business was now in the hands of only one of the original owners that it was sold to a larger firm. Even though I was no longer a part of the firm by this time, it was nice to see it have the longevity that it did.

I was fortunate in that while I did not leave Sprint in the best of circumstances from my perspective, I did not burn any bridges behind me. I made some contacts, and I was able to return to the company in December of 1998 and bridge my service time. I became a Project Manager for major business customers. I coordinated internal and subcontractor resources, assured product delivery schedules and coordinated all project activities to meet implementation deadlines and profitability goals. Since the company had gone through some changes, there was a brief amount of time spent in the **Initiation** and **Integration Phases**. The **Transition Phase** was virtually non-existent for me, and I moved into the **Leadership Phase** rather quickly.

My success again brought me to a place of developing another area of the business. In 2002 I became Program Manager for all aspects of contractor management for Sprint's business and wholesale markets organization nationwide. I had to build a totally new master contractor program including development of performance measures, cost-saving performance improvements and standard practices and procedures. The big job I had to tackle was the consolidation of contractor resources from somewhere in excess of 400 contractors nationwide down to 25 total national and regional contractors. All objectives were met and exceeded, and my efforts were recognized and rewarded with two coveted *Sprint Values Excellence* awards.

In 2004 I took on another new role as Technical Engineering Supervisor to put together a team of technical engineers supporting new wireless business customer implementations for the eastern half of the

United States. I defined and developed the role of the team which provided application and configuration of devices as well as technical support for large business customers.

This role then evolved into Manager—Program/Project Management as we undertook all program/project management duties supporting large business wireless deployment projects for the eastern half of the country. The challenge I faced and delivered on was to develop a team of technical engineers into program/project managers.

While I felt good about my career development along the way, I felt like I really brought it all together with this extremely successful team. We handled some very large projects including rolling out wireless solutions for UPS, the United States Census Bureau, Kodak, KPMG, Merck, BASF and many others.

The culmination of my efforts were recognized when I was nominated for and accepted into Sprint's *Leadership Excellence* program. This program not only recognized the top leaders in the company, but also provided some high-level training with industry experts in leadership. Fewer than 20 individuals were accepted into this program company-wide (which included nearly 60,000 employees at the time).

Like a lot of people, I had dreams of an early retirement from about the age of 50. Unfortunately, the collapse of the technology market in 2000 had a profound effect upon my assets as I was over-committed in technology stocks.

Not long into this final position of my career at Sprint, I once again had thoughts of an early retirement. My successful career allowed me to take advantage of the opportunity to take an early retirement in 2007. I would say that it was late-2005/early-2006 when I had officially found myself in the **Legacy Phase** of my career. I had a well-functioning team, and I saw high-promise for some of them to advance their own careers. I truly felt I had grown into and had been a good servant-leader in my career. I had been recognized in my performance reviews numerous times throughout my career for my communications skills, organization, teamwork, integrity and commitment to values. It is in these attributes that I hope I left my personal legacy.

During this time I also found myself thinking more and more about what I would do after retirement. My thoughts always went to some of the hobbies I had pursued in my life. I would now have the time to really "work" on those hobbies. That is exactly what I have done since retiring. But, I also found one other large activity that gained in prominence, and that is being a grandfather. This is a most fun and rewarding activity for sure!

Appendix 3 - Faith Background

I have included a bit about my growth in faith as I did with the background on my personal career. And as with my personal career background, it is certainly included not to puff up my ego in any way. In fact, it was a long time before I took a real interest in faith. I did pray occasionally as a child, but it was mostly out of a selfish fear of being caught at something. I am not proud of some of the rough beginnings of my journey, and it has been a challenging journey for me at times. Maybe it is really not so different than the experiences of many.

I can remember walking to a church near the neighborhood where we lived. It was 1953, and I was about five years old. I apparently was in a Sunday school class as I can recall sitting at a desk in a classroom-like setting. The one clear image I have retained is a picture on the wall of Jesus with a lamb around his shoulders. I do not recall any childhood church experiences other than this. The next few times I recall being in a church were for funerals. Sundays for me throughout my childhood were for sleeping late, watching Sunday cartoons and kids' shows, and reading comics in the Sunday papers.

I can only recall my father saying something about the church only wanting his money. I am not sure if there was some particular incident that created this. I also know that his father, my grandfather, did not attend church either. My grandmother, on the other hand, did attend the Methodist Church on a regular basis and was involved in many church activities. I can also remember my mother attending church a few times without us.

My next actual church experience as best as I can recall was sometime after graduating from high school; I truly do not know exactly when this was. Unfortunately, it was not a good experience on my part. I do not like sharing this story, but I am being open about myself and my growth as a Christ follower, so here goes.

I had been dating my wife-to-be for some time. She was Catholic. She had asked me numerous times to attend church with her, but I had always refused. I had been drinking one Saturday evening, and still she asked me to go to church with her. So, in my weakened state, I agreed to go. I made a complete fool of myself mocking the kneeling and the standing and singing too loudly. I am surprised that she did not dump me right then and there. But, I guess God works in mysterious ways as he had other plans.

I am sure I attended church with my future wife a few more times in the intervening years up to 1970. I had to make up for my stupidity after all. In 1970 when I was a senior in college, I asked her to marry me. Since it was to be a Catholic wedding, we would need to attend marriage preparation classes. We took the classes together on campus when she would come to visit me on week-ends. I think it was fortunate for me to be studying with a college campus priest as he understood my age group very well. My interest in the faith grew through this process, and my church attendance increased.

After my graduation in 1971, we moved to Warsaw, Indiana, and I went to work for United Telephone Company of Indiana. Upon settling in Warsaw I took lessons on the Catholic faith and joined the Catholic Church. One reason for my decision was that I felt it important to worship together as a family, and we had our first child in December of that year. While I had been baptized as a baby, I did make a conditional baptism in the Catholic Church ... just in case the first one didn't take.

We continued in the Catholic faith through our adult years, and we were very involved in church activities. With the growth of our faith, we became involved in the right-to-life movement from its very inception. I served as treasurer and then president of our local county organization. We also assisted with a local pregnancy center that helped women choose life.

Our involvement in faith issues led me into becoming a member of our parish council for several years. I also taught religion classes to middle school students for several years. As part of my plan to overcome my fear of public speaking while serving in the church, I became a lector and read the Sunday Bible readings before the congregation.

Since I had no real religious upbringing, the Catholic Church was good for me. The heavy rules and regulations were just what I needed to help me learn about my faith and to keep me in line. I will not say that I was the best Catholic, but I did what I could to learn and to serve.

It was also through the church that I became involved in ParentShare, a mentoring program for adults. I mentored a single father of three teenage girls. That in itself would be enough for anyone! But, he was also very poor; he worked nights at the local sewage plant in a very thankless job. I assisted him with managing his daughters and his finances and his outlook on life. It was one of the most difficult and rewarding things I have ever done. I have stayed in touch with him to this day.

As our kids became adults with their own families, we both grew away from the Catholic Church. For both of us, the continued revelations of child abuse by priests were too overwhelming. I had been having thoughts of leaving the church even before that, however. I was finding that while all those rules and regulations had been good for me in my early development as a Christian, those things were now getting in the way of spirituality for me. The focus seemed to me to be more on the rules than on living a spirit-filled life. I needed a change.

We had attended a small local community church, Warsaw Community Church, that our oldest son had been attending and serving in as a musician. We eventually made this our new home for church sometime around or just after 2000. It has been very spiritually uplifting for me personally. My wife sometimes still misses what she refers to as the reverence of the Catholic Church. Our daughter and her family attend this same church as well. We have met new friends and participate regularly in a small group that formed during a larger study we participated in through the church.

We aren't as actively involved in this church as we had once been. Part of that, I think, has to do with age and family. When your kids are small, there is a tendency to be involved in their activities, including church activities. This was especially true in the Catholic Church as it also had a grade school that our children attended. As I mentioned, we do participate in a small group Bible study. Engaging with our small group and sharing our life experience with some younger members feels right. These small groups are important as the small community church has grown to nearly 3,000 members.

Appendix 4 - Personal Vision and Values

My personal vision and values statement was developed in 1992. I had moved into a new position developing a new area of business, and I was voraciously reading everything I could find on the topics of innovation and entrepreneurship. It was during this time that I developed my personal vision and values after working on the same for my team. I was under a lot of (self-)pressure at the time to perform. Developing my personal vision and values helped me to be better grounded. I cannot recall at this time which book or books I read that pushed me in this direction. I have listed several good books in the **Bibliography and References** list that I was reading about this time. I had also attended some management and leadership development seminars around this same time.

I feel that the idea of mission, vision and values is an evolution of developing your goals. Goals can be very specific, definable and short-term (in the larger picture). They are typically more tactical in nature during your early career development. Your manager will have strategic goals to work towards. In your early career, your tactical goals will help your manager achieve her strategic goals. At higher management levels, you will be more directly involved in developing strategic goals and assuring their attainment.

As businesses grew and competition became stronger, businesses needed to differentiate themselves to be more competitive. One means to this end was to define the mission of the business to let both the employees and the public know who they were. A mission statement defines who you are now and what you have to offer. Your personal mission at work will be very closely tied to your current position. The goals you establish with your manager are very likely supporting your mission. For example, part of your mission might be to be the best (fill-in-the-blank) in the company. As you achieve the goals that you and your manager have established, you will be supporting that mission.

To further enhance their positions, the businesses developed their vision and values statements. This provided them with an underlying foundation for the culture that drives the soul of the company. The vision of your company tells you and others why the business exists. The values of the company tells you and others who the company is.

In the same way, you need to have a firm foundation upon which to develop your personal career. In doing so, you really need to do some soul-searching. What is the vision of who you are and who you want to be? And, remember, you cannot be two people. You are one individual who has one vision for your life. This is not the vision for your job; it is the vision for you singly and fully as one unique creation of God. You must next understand the values you live by, or those you want to live by, and clearly communicate those in some simple values statements.

This is a process that takes time and some healthy and honest self-analysis. A simple search on the internet will turn up plenty of tools to assist you with this task. There are some very clear definitions for mission and vision and values. There are good study guides and workbooks to help you develop your personal vision and values. This is worth taking the time to do. I obviously did not do this early in my career as it was not even a topic at the time. But, when I saw the opportunity and the value it had for my personal and professional growth, I was all in.

I had not pulled out my personal vision and values statement and reviewed it for quite a few years. At one time I did have it hanging on the wall in my home office. Through some moves it was packed away in a box. Pulling it out as I began to organize this book, it spoke to me as if I had just developed it yesterday. I was glad to see that it had met the test of time and still serves me well. I do not know if your own statement will serve you for the next 10 years or 20 years or 30 years, but review it regularly and update it as necessary to reflect the changes in you or your circumstances. Keep it somewhere where you can reflect on it at regular intervals. It is a valuable guidepost.

My personal vision and values statement from November 1992 appears exactly as originally written on the next page.

Personal Vision and Values
of
Jim Barber

Vision

Use the gifts and talents with which the Lord has blessed me to the benefit of my family, my friends, my neighbors, and my vocation, and experience internal peace and outward joy in living my life.

Values

- *Seek daily guidance and renewal from God.*
- *Know the joy of living. Realize that God has created us to experience all of life, both the "ups" and the "downs."*
- *Don't try so hard. Use my faith to get me through the "downs" and to say thank-you for the "ups."*
- *Take care of my physical, mental, and spiritual health.*
- *My family is one of God's greatest gifts; they affirm His care and love. Enjoy this gift and care for it well.*
- *Care and nurture my extended work family. Maintain a balance in life to ensure that I do not burn out through overwork.*
- *Respect ... myself, others, differences.*
- *Integrity.*
- *Love.*

Bibliography and References

Note 1:

Biblical references are noted throughout the book, and in line with the Chicago Manual Style guidelines, they do not appear in the bibliography. Several different translations have been used in the interest of providing a bit of diversity. As I personally use a New International Version (NIV) bible, that translation appears more than most others, and it is listed below. Additionally, an on-line resource, Bible Gateway, was used to review various translations, and it is also listed in the references. All translations other than from NIV were sourced using the Bible Gateway website. Translations used in the book include:

ESV (English Standard Version)
GNT (Good News Translation)
ISV (International Standard Version)
KJV (King James Version)
NASB (New American Standard Bible)
NET (New English Translation)
NIV (New International Version)
NLT (New Living Translation)
NRSV (New Revised Standard Version)
TLB (The Living Bible)

Note 2:

Some of the books listed here may not be directly referenced in this book. I have included several books that influenced me in my career and which I feel remain relevant in their topic area. These are some of the readings that influenced me and whose ideas have surely worked their way into this book. Thus this section is the Bibliography and References, *and* a reading list. Yes, I am very aware that there are other more contemporary books and authors who offer much relevancy for today. Read them! Topics of goal-setting, servant-leadership, integrity, honesty and other topics that are basic to your career management are as relevant today as they were 20-25 years ago.

Adler, Ronald B., Lawrence B. Rosenfeld and Russell F. Proctor. 2001. *Interplay: The Process of Interpersonal Communicating*, 8th edition. Fort Worth: Harcourt.

Albrecht, Karl, and Ron Zemke. 1990. *Service America!* New York: Warner Books.

Barker, Kenneth L., general editor. 2011. *The Holy Bible, New International Version*. Grand Rapids: Zondervan.

Bible Gateway. 2014. https://www.biblegateway.com/passage/. Accessed 2014-2015. All translations other than NIV were sourced through Bible Gateway.

Blanchard, Kenneth H., and Mark Miller. 2012. *Great Leaders Grow*. San Francisco: Berrett-Koehler.

Blanchard, Kenneth H., and Spencer Johnson. 1982. *One-Minute Manager*. New York: Morrow.

Bosak, Susan V. 2000. "What Is Legacy?" *The Legacy Project*. www.legacyproject.org/guides/whatislegacy.html. Accessed February 2015.

Branson, Richard. 2015. *My First 90 Days: Founding 400 Companies Feels Like Starting 400 New Jobs*. LinkedIn. https://www.linkedin.com/pulse/my-first-90-days-founding-400-companies-feels-like-starting-branson. Accessed January 2015.

Brennfleck, Kevin, and Kay Marie Brennfleck. 2005. *Live Your Calling*. San Francisco: Jossey-Bass.

Bridges, William. 2009. *Managing Transitions*. Philadelphia: Da Capo Press.

Bruce, Alexander B. 1871. *The Training of the Twelve*. Edinburgh: T. &T. Clark. Kindle edition.

Bureau of Labor Statistics, U.S. Department of Labor. 2014. *Employee Tenure in 2014.* USDL-14-1714. http://www.bls.gov/news.release/pdf/tenure.pdf. Accessed November 2014.

Carnegie, Dale. 1981. *How to Win Friends and Influence People.* New York: Simon & Schuster.

Cecere, Lora. 2015. *My First 90 Days: Listen to What is Not Said.* LinkedIn. https://www.linkedin.com/pulse/my-first-90-days-listen-what-said-lora-cecere. Accessed January 2015.

Chopra, Deepak. 2015. *My First 90 Days: Master Self-Care First Before Diving Into a New Job.* LinkedIn. https://www.linkedin.com/pulse/my-first-90-days-master-self-care-before-diving-new-deepak. Accessed January 2015.

Collins, Jim. 2001. *Good to Great.* New York: HarperCollins Publishers, Inc.

Covey, Stephen R. 1989. *The 7 Habits of Highly Effective People.* New York: Simon & Schuster.

Covey, Stephen R. 1994. *First Things First.* New York: Simon & Schuster.

Croston, Glenn. 2012. "The Thing We Fear More Than Death." *Psychology Today.* https://www.psychologytoday.com/blog/the-real-story-risk/201211/the-thing-we-fear-more-death. Accessed January 2015.

Dickens, Charles. [date of publication not identified]. *A Tale of Two Cities.* Garden City: Nelson Doubleday, Inc.

Gallo, Amy. 2014. "4 Things You Thought Were True About Time Management." *Harvard Business Review.* July 22, 2014. hbr.org/2014/07/4-things-you-thought-were-true-about-time-management/. Accessed January 2015.

Geerdens, Inge. 2015. *My First 90 Days: Accept That You Can't Change the World in 3 Months.* LinkedIn. https://www.linkedin.com/pulse/my-first-90-days-accept-you-cant-change-world-3-months-inge-geerdens. Accessed January 2015.

Greenleaf, Robert K. 1970. "What is Servant Leadership?" from *The Servant as a Leader.* The Robert K. Greenleaf Center for Servant Leadership. https://greenleaf.org/what-is-servant-leadership/. Accessed February 2015.

Hall-Flavin, Daniel K. "How Can I Overcome My Fear of Public Speaking?" Mayo Clinic. http://www.mayoclinic.org/diseases-conditions/phobias/expert-answers/fear-of-public-speaking/faq-20058416. Accessed January 2015.

Hebrew for Christians. 2015. www.hebrew4christians.com. Accessed January 2105.

Judaism 101. 2015. www.jewfaq.org. Accessed January 2105.

Maxwell, John C. 2007. *Be a People Person.* Colorado Springs: David C Cook.

McBirnie, William Steuart. 2004. *The Search for the Twelve Apostles,* revised edition. Carol Stream: Tyndale House.

Merriam-Webster Online Dictionary. 2015. Merriam-Webster, Incorporated. http://www.merriam-webster.com. Accessed 2014-2015.

Ortberg, John. 2008. *Faith and Doubt.* Grand Rapids: Zondervan.

Peters, Thomas J. 1995. *Pursuit of Wow!* London: Macmillan.

Peters, Thomas J., and Robert H. Waterman. 1982. *In Search of Excellence: Lessons from America's Best-Run Companies.* New York: Harper & Row.

Peters, Thomas J., and Nancy Austin. 1985. *A Passion for Excellence: The Leadership Difference.* New York: Random House.

Peters, Thomas J. 1987. *Thriving on Chaos: Handbook for a Manage-*

ment Revolution. New York: Knopf.

RW Research, Inc. 2004. *The Twelve Disciples*. Torrance: Rose Publishing.

Sanborn, Mark. 2004. *The Fred Factor*. New York: Doubleday.

Tardanico, Susan. 2012. "Five Ways to Make Peace with Failure." *Forbes*.
http://www.forbes.com/sites/susantardanico/2012/09/27/five-ways-to-make-peace-with-failure/. Accessed February 2015.

Thalheimer, Will. 2010. *How Much Do People Forget?* http://www.-work-learning.com/catalog.html. Accessed January 2015.

Thesaurus.com. *Roget's 21st Century Thesaurus, Third Edition*. 2009. Philip Lief Group. http://www.thesaurus.com/. Accessed 2014-2015.

Warren, Rick. 2002. *The Purpose Driven Life*. Grand Rapids: Zondervan.

Index